MW00809367

About the Author

Kat Seeber, MD is a primary care doctor in nursing homes, initially trained in the Navy. No sooner did she start medical school than she was diagnosed with a cancer that threatened her life, legs, and medical career. The path that followed proved to be a Kafka-esque series of events and trials that would take her to the very brink. Through perseverance, grit, love, and humor, her path of survival, medicine, and motherhood took shape. It has been a catastrophic journey that led to all that any of us really need: hope.

Dedication

To Cam and Casey, the loves of my life who give me the strength to push through every day.

To my parents, who protected and supported Casey when I couldn't, and who inspired in me the will to fight.

To my brother, whose kindness and gentle guitar helped soothe the fear and hopelessness with love.

And to Avery, Sara, and Pat, who have helped me win the fight against myself so far.

Kat Seeber, MD

THE GIFT OF HOPE

AUSTIN MACAULEY PUBLISHERS™

LONDON • CAMBRIDGE • NEW YORK • SHARJAH

Copyright © Kat Seeber, MD 2024

All rights reserved. No part of this publication may be reproduced, distributed, or transmitted in any form or by any means, including photocopying, recording, or other electronic or mechanical methods, without the prior written permission of the publisher, except in the case of brief quotations embodied in critical reviews and certain other non-commercial uses permitted by copyright law. For permission requests, write to the publisher.

Any person who commits any unauthorized act in relation to this publication may be liable to criminal prosecution and civil claims for damages.

All of the events in this memoir are true to the best of author's memory. The views expressed in this memoir are solely those of the author.

Ordering Information
Quantity sales: Special discounts are available on quantity purchases by corporations, associations, and others. For details, contact the publisher at the address below.

Publisher's Cataloging-in-Publication data
Seeber, MD, Kat
The Gift of Hope

ISBN 9798891551077 (Paperback)
ISBN 9798891551084 (Hardback)
ISBN 9798891551107 (ePub e-book)
ISBN 9798891551091 (Audiobook)

Library of Congress Control Number: 2023920992

www.austinmacauley.com/us

First Published 2024
Austin Macauley Publishers LLC
40 Wall Street, 33rd Floor, Suite 3302
New York, NY 10005
USA

mail-usa@austinmacauley.com
+1 (646) 5125767

Acknowledgment

Thank you, Mom, Esther, Keith, Rob, Danara, Christina, Casey, and Cam for helping me to shape the narrative and for appreciating the value of the fight. I wouldn't have had the courage to share my path if it were not for you.

Table of Contents

In 90 minutes, all of the frustration of having my pain, fear, persistence, suffering, and medical decisions questioned and minimized for 17 years was wiped away. I paid out of pocket since my recently renewed lack of leg function has been progressing and disregarded by my doctor. A pre-eminent neuro-oncologist on my specific, rare, neurologic cancer validated it all in just one conversation. Her appreciation for me living the impossible and defying seemingly insurmountable odds up to this point evaporated all of the tears of feeling misunderstood. And she simultaneously offered me the hope of cure and future that I have been desperate for, for almost two decades. I feel free.

Diagnosis

In 2005, I was in my first few months of medical school at the joint service medical school just outside DC. I was born and raised in DC and never knew it existed until I was applying to medical school. I had recently become a Navy wife (for the first time), which is all but comical in the context of my upbringing, and the military commitment no longer seemed foreign. I had grown to appreciate the value and honor of military service, and getting paid to go to medical school sounded like a fantastic plan.

I suffered from severe back pain radiating down my legs in Officer Indoctrination School before matriculation, but since I had recently run a sprint triathlon, they assumed that it was a femur fracture in a young, thin white woman. The MRI they did at the time stopped less than a centimeter below the real culprit and didn't find anything of concern. When school started, I immediately dove into academics and fell in love with medicine more and more by the day. I pushed through classes and periodically sought care at the school clinic. It felt like the nerves in my legs were being pulled on like drawstrings. I could trace them all. The pain was indescribable, but nothing had been found, so I made it through.

Eventually, they ordered an MRI of my lower back. I joked as I left study group the afternoon of October 30, 2005 (on my way to the scan) that I either had a slipped disc or a tumor and that I would let them know tomorrow.

The MRI should have been 30 minutes or so. It was my first MRI, so the claustrophobia was hard to contain, but I just focused on breathing and told myself it felt longer than it was. After an hour and a half or so, they brought me out to secure my head for a brain MRI and give me contrast.

"Where is it?" I asked.

"I can't talk about it. You'll have to wait for the radiologist report," said the MRI tech.

"You found a mass. Where is it?"

"I can't tell you that."

"You wouldn't be giving me contrast if you hadn't found something. Where, in my spine?"

"The filum terminale."

"In the middle of the cauda equina? Does it involve the conus of the spinal cord?"

Total panic on the tech's face. "You're in medicine?"

"Med student."

The expletive was implied. They weren't supposed to tell me.

"It's time to go back in," they said.

"Okay." My mind swam with the logistics of surgery for a small benign mass that would explain my pain. I hadn't the slightest idea what was really to come.

When the scan was done, they took out the IV, asked me to get dressed, and told me to be at the chief of neurosurgery's office the following morning at 07:30. I drove home recalling the irony of my departure from study group. I hadn't yet grappled with why they needed to image my entire spinal column and brain.

I was new to medicine, but I knew I would not remember the words said the next day and that my family would complicate the matter if they came with me. I called a longtime friend in DC with a history of medical education. She was stoic, reliable, honest, and could be brutal when necessary. She was perfect. She agreed to be my reporter and came the next day equipped with a notepad.

When they called us back, we met with the neurosurgery resident. He seemed to be whispering at me. My friend and I exchanged glances. Surgery was in six days. I can only remember snippets.

"You have 100% chance of total lower extremity paralysis. You have a mass encompassing your cauda equina."

"Try to save my legs."

"You aren't hearing me. You'll never touch your toes or tie your shoes again."

"I understand. Try to save my legs if you can."

"You aren't hearing me. There is no saving your legs."

"I do understand. I'm just asking you to try. Don't scrape the nerves. Leave some in if you have to."

He was flustered. He thought I wasn't getting it. I suppose I wasn't. But I was looking for hope. So he showed us the scan. He emphasized that they were shocked it didn't show up in my brain.

I was only a few months into med school. I had little experience with radiology at that point, other than maybe chest X-rays.

"I don't see it."

"It's right there," he said, pointing.

"Where?"

"Right there."

"It's all white. I don't see the mass."

"That whole thing is the mass."

I turned and looked at my friend. A tear was rolling down her cheek. I don't know that I had ever seen her cry in the 16 years we had been close friends. *Fuck* was all I could think. There was a huge mass from just below my spinal cord. It was wrapped around every spinal nerve to my legs.

For the next six days, I briefed friends and family. I took out my 'bone box' from school and showed my family where, and how extensive, the tumor was. I went to dinner at places where a wheelchair wouldn't fit. I joked about all the ways we would spruce up my wheels. It hadn't occurred to me that it wasn't benign, though the fact that they were so concerned about my brain gnawed at me.

My then husband took an emergency flight to DC. He was still stationed in San Diego. We went through the motions of trying to reconcile what was happening, but each moment was filled with numbness or logistics of how to live paralyzed. I hadn't even begun to question living.

I told the school that I understood I would be kicked out. I was devastated but tried to be stoic. To my amazement, they said that they would see how surgery went first and then make decisions. They were happy to support my struggle and give me time to recover. I still can't believe it. But I was grateful for the slim chance while confident of the inevitable. My life and dreams as I knew them, as I had fought for through my life of dedication to academics, high school cum laude, dean's list at Cornell, nonprofit work to provide for low-income seniors, the homeless needs assessment I did personally and secured funding for at city council, the schizophrenia study I volunteered and worked at, the multiple jobs while volunteering. They had all led me here and it was all about to go away with my legs.

My best friend flew in for the surgery. She passed out in the bathroom while awaiting the results of the 12-hour surgery. She didn't even tell anyone. While I was blissfully anesthetized, my family and friends fought through the excruciating hours.

The Surgery

I remember about 30 minutes of the next few days. Pressing the button every three minutes. My then husband counting down between each button push. The knowledge of agony. Hearing him say "head down!" every time I inadvertently moved. I was supposed to stay still for three days so as not to further traumatize my nerves. A vague recollection of vomiting in a bucket after anesthesia without being allowed to move. People rushing in to cart me off to a CT after my oxygen dropped suddenly. Screaming "my back!" over each bump and hearing the staff and my then husband scream "we know!" back at me. The terror of being moved.

In all honesty, I feel for the staff and my then husband in those moments. I've been on both sides of it. We do know. But things might get real bad if we don't get the scan. I very well might have formed clots in my lungs after such a major surgery. I had to suck it up. I think that's one of the main reasons I am the way I am as a doc. There's a big difference between "we know and we're being very careful. We really need to make sure that your scan is okay," and "we know!" angrily shouted, but I digress.

Days passed. My neurosurgeon and the senior neurosurgical resident appeared at the bottom of my bed. "It's time," they said. "Try to wiggle your toes." I did, and floored that I could, I bent my knees to see if more worked. Everyone screamed "NO" in unison. I would undo their work if I moved too much.

From there, at least an odd remembrance of temporary serenity. Hope of walking. The pain continued, but in the context of hope, it was far more sustainable. PT showed up. They brought a wheelchair.

"I'm not getting in it."

"What do you mean, you have to."

"I'll never get out. No." A look of confusion.

"Tell him what you want me to do. I'll do it. You don't want to have to deal with how stubborn I am. Trust me."

From there, I just remember dragging my legs for loop after loop around the nurse's station with the walker. It was excruciating. Many of my muscles no longer worked. I could barely feel half of each leg. More than a foot of my back had been ripped out, spine removed, just to get at the mass. But I could do step by step, and so I did. Rounds and rounds a day. Determination mattered more than pain. After six days, I pled to be discharged very much against my neurosurgeon's wishes.

"You can't do stairs."

"It's on the first floor."

That's all I got. I just remember pushing and somehow winning. The school called me after I got back to my apartment. They were going to visit me, but thought I would be inpatient for weeks or more. They somehow missed me. I said I was home and doing well doing self-PT and had PT scheduled outpatient at the hospital. They told me I had 30 days leave, plus extra for Christmas break. We would see how it went come the new semester.

I had 25 staples in my back, if I recall. I had to roll like a log a couple of times a night because not moving made the pain worse. I had to wake up my then husband to roll me. I was exceptionally stubborn about showers and going to the bathroom. I remember the indignity. At least three times a day I would try to stretch, and then the PT I could tolerate every couple hours. After not long, whatever that means, I started walking on the treadmill at my apartment complex. Progressively, I got to a mile a day.

After 30 days and the staples out prior, I was allowed to go in the water. My then husband and I went to the gym. I swam a mile. Swimming had always been the most difficult in training for sprints. As we left the gym that first day, we ran into the senior neurosurgical resident on my case. As we were getting ready to go, I said hello. "It's a hell of a lot easier to swim a mile without a tumor in your back."

He didn't think it was funny. He was furious. "Do you know how worried about you I was!" He stormed off. My then husband went to the changing room to talk to him.

All I could feel was hope and achievement. I did feel a little bad, but not really. I couldn't believe it either.

Back to School

Long and short, it hurt. Up for hours at a time was agony. I lay on the carpet in the back of the auditorium, in uniform, listening to lectures. No chance I could sit for that long. I missed a lot of classes, studied in bed, and did my PT. I kept progressing. My professors were incredibly understanding and I went to all labs. I had missed biochemistry, but I studied on my own and made it up over the summer. I missed saying goodbye to my grandfather to take the test. I sent him a letter through my mom before he passed, telling him I loved him and that it was okay to let go. He squeezed her hand. I stayed focused.

Anatomy lab was the hardest. Dissecting, labeling, sitting on a stool: pain. My lab partner was amazing. His son had leukemia and we shared an oncologist. When I was still inpatient, we met in the waiting room one day. His son was there for treatment. I was there to find out what mine was. There was a bond.

We talked about the day we met in the waiting room, how the oncology resident dictated to me that I would start radiation the next day. My then husband nodded. I said "no."

"You only had partial resection of a very malignant cancer. Radiation starts tomorrow."

"But that will kill my ovaries. I'm not ready."

"Yes, it will, and there's no other choice."

"I need to freeze eggs. I want a child."

"Well, no, you won't be able to have a child."

"Then, no."

"I'll get my staff," said the resident.

My then husband agreed with the resident, but I wanted a kid. I had not yet processed that I had cancer. I focused on still having my legs, and stubbornly clung to still having a full life. When the staff came in, he was seemingly very honest. "It's a very rare cancer and we don't know much about it. You can wait and we can see what a scan looks like in three months and then we can go from there." Agreed. Time to think, plan for freezing eggs, absorb the situation, and go from there.

For years, I had dreams of being overtaken by a tidal wave in the days before my scans. It would be massive, crash onto me, and I would discover that I could breathe under water. I still felt suffocated and overwhelmingly anxious, but it means something different to me now than it did then. The three-month MRI was clear. No visible evidence of cancer. It was out of this world, still is.

So Mark and I would sit by the cadaver, dissecting many things that I had just had dissected, and we would talk about his son's leukemia and my cancer. His son kept fighting. I was in an observation period. Neither of us could make head or tail of it.

He dissected, I labeled. I never would have made it through if it wasn't for him. My back was excruciating just sitting. They cut open over a foot of my back, L1-S2 hemilaminectomies just to get at the cancer, further consequences to come. Bending over a body wasn't doable. So he did it, and we talked our way through cancer. We both passed the class.

Years later, he died by suicide. We had lost touch, though I am not drawing a connection there. But I do wish we could have had one of those soul-baring talks before he did what he did.

"In You, It's Recurrence"

School kept going. I wasn't really okay. I was great when filling my minutes with medicine. Studying, considering the impact to people's lives, ferreting out the differential diagnosis and testing process. Building my clinical acumen. Putting my angst to work. But in the moments where I wasn't studying or working, the terror reigned. I found it nearly impossible to have normal everyday conversations, to exist in the mundane. Either I was short on time here or I was in awe of the fact that I was being allowed to stay here. I couldn't really cope with either.

But I pressed on. Purpose. Distraction. The nuance of medicine. I was doing it against all odds. I was walking. And then the leg drag started. It wasn't even really that painful, I don't think. Not beyond the usual. I would just try to get my remaining muscles to function and they wouldn't respond. Straight to my neurosurgeon. The same resident saw me. "Could be a number of things, but in you, it's recurrence."

The echo in my brain. I should've known better than to hope this much. I should have known I wouldn't get away without radiation, that my legs wouldn't last. I shouldn't have dared hope.

But the scan was clear. The scar tissue had formed weird collections of fluid around the nerves. It looked like knotted string. So, was I going to be paralyzed by surgery, not cancer? Was it cancer? Is it cancer? Is there anything we can do?

Tap the fluid. That was the plan. Interventional radiology would stick needles in the pockets, draw out fluid, see if there was more cancer in the fluid, and go from there. It wasn't reassuring, but it was a plan. Moving forward, whatever that meant.

The interventional radiologist looked like Billy Bob Thornton. He was a great guy. Kind. Cerebral. Congenial. So I laid on the table, ass up, needles ready, imaging arm hovering above, him in his lead vest.

So, this is where it gets funny. We were in the basement of Bethesda Naval Hospital. My then husband sitting in the hall. A pedal at Billy Bob Thornton's feet. Every time he needed an image of the needle position, he would step on the pedal...and the lights would flicker. It was around the same time Walter Reed Hospital was falling down, and apparently, there was some sort of electrical incongruence. But I swear to God, the lights would flicker.

Not only that, but the scar tissue that was forming around my nerves, creating these pockets, kept my nerves from floating away from the needle in the cerebrospinal fluid (CSF) in my spinal column, so he would skewer the nerves. Every time he pushed the needle in, I screamed in agony the location of the nerve distribution he was skewering. Over and over. Must've been 20 taps or more, or at least 20 adjustments with the associated scream diagnosing the nerve distribution of the skewered nerve.

"Kat, I'm so sorry. But this is one of the coolest things I've ever seen," with a chuckle.

"It's ok," I said. "It's pretty damn cool to be able to describe it." We both laughed.

Tap, tap, tap. Scream, scream, scream. Fluid removed, cysts decompressed, legs working again, cytology negative.

Not only could I walk again, but I didn't have cancer again. Back to work. Long hours, hard work, getting muscles back, building my medical brain. I just kept going.

It was about nine months from my initial surgery to the first leg drag…after learning to walk again. The next time it was only six months. Tap, tap, tap. Scream, scream, scream. Cytology negative. Legs worked again. Then three months or so. Chasing my dream was literally scarring me with the long hours and hard work. Living my life was taking my legs. And it was time to start clinical rotations, no more studying in bed.

The Clinical Years

My clinical years were a godsend. I was still in my 20s. My friends and family needed to believe that my fight was over. That I had won. Living like that was too much. Too much fear, too much uncertainty, too much energy. But I had come to believe that you don't beat cancer until you die of something else. I was racked by it.

I was trying to learn to sit with my uncertainty, to take the sting out. I wanted to live. But I had lost the illusion of immortality, and I found it very difficult to pretend that I believed I was going to be okay. I tried to get used to being 'okay for now'. I tried to take the good days and months and learn to be content with them. But I was far from it. I'm far from it even now, though I have learned to accept some of the peace that gratitude for the unknown can bring.

But in medicine, I found that the people actively undergoing one crisis or another, one fear or another, relished in having a provider who acknowledged the unknown and parsed it into digestible pieces, some of them even with solutions or treatment. I learned the art of facing the unknown and creating a path, little by little, always striving for forward. And when there was no forward, I would cry with them. Even when there was forward, I would cry with them. I learned to sit with the beast that is cancer in the room with me, and to hold the hands of my patients as they did the same.

If that sounds grandiosely simple, you are correct. It has not been, and never will be, simple. It hurt. It hurt A LOT. It still does. But piece by piece I learned not to run from it. I've always been somewhat grotesquely honest about the hard stuff. I've smoothed the edges a bit over the last 18 years, but I've also learned to spot the ones that want to hear the hard truth, and those who need more time.

I remember the first patient that I diagnosed with cancer. It was the third year of medical school and I was on the wards. I believe we saw it on CT, no biopsy yet. But it was evident. And I asked if I could tell her. My resident nervously allowed me, and stood by for the first part of the conversation to see if I had it in me. I did. I managed not to cry until I left the room. And then I walked to the end of the hallway, buried my head in my hands, and wept. I could feel the monster I knew in my words. I could feel the inevitability, my own inevitability, and there was no chasing it away.

And then, after choking down the sobs, I got to work. Teach me. What were the symptoms likely to be? What could be mollified? How could we improve quality of life and for how long? There was no avoiding the road. No denying it. But how do we navigate it? And my own journey, still winding, fueled my fire. I knew we were powerless against this same monster, but where could we find power while it tightened its grip? My future and so much of my life was borne in that moment.

I stopped holding back tears when they wanted to come. I learned to cry with people, to acknowledge their fear and rage. To let it unravel a moment before setting out choices for the path. It turned out that it applied to so many things, not just cancer. I learned to acknowledge the unknown and dive into the investigations. I kept my patients informed along the way. I learned the power of being honest about what wasn't known, and how to lay out for them that we would try to figure it out together. My calling was clear.

There were plenty of other patients. Clear-cut, simple, easy interventions and cures and diagnoses. And I enjoyed them. But the hard ones have always been my passion. "I don't know." I've never been afraid to say it to my patients, and I've never trusted a doc who is afraid to say it to me. So much power lies in understanding what you don't know, and then trying to figure out what aspects are unknowable and what pieces can be figured out.

I don't know that there is anything incredible about that. In fact, I insist there isn't. But it is also uncommon. The relief in my patients' faces when I am willing to acknowledge the uncertainty has been obvious. And the subsequent fear inevitable. I haven't shared with all of them my similar fight. There is a subset that wants to hear it while others feel the need to continue the delusion of immortality.

It's always a risk to relay my fight in effort to validate the humanity of it all.

NIH

As part of my training and internal medicine journey, I was assigned a terminal patient across the street at NIH, instructed to delve into her battle. It was a singularly rewarding experience. I know not everyone felt that way. To many it was a burden, a check in the box. And it was then that I learned that healthcare would be a much more human place if doctors learned to suffer like their patients. I hadn't chosen it, but I refused to run away from it. I dove in.

She had metastatic breast cancer, an incredibly loving husband, and all the resources in the world. But, unfortunately, she had little to no chance of surviving. We didn't have monoclonal antibodies yet. Radiation had failed and chemo was failing. She had a number of beautiful wigs. Over the time that we knew each other, she stopped wearing them. The wigs became a symbol of denial to her and she was desperately trying to wrestle with the impossible reality of impending death.

I spent hours in her room. We talked about our lives and all the things we thought we were guaranteed, the diminishing hope that they were. I researched all the new things happening that might help her, knowing that her doctors were experts and I was a mere med student. But we talked about the possibility of hope. Of the guilt that our families had to suffer for us. Of how a person is to soothe the ones whom will outlive them.

We talked on the phone for years. And then the calls became sparse. She was declining, mostly bed-bound now. And then the calls stopped. She had surpassed expectations, but reality came to bear. And there was no call. No notice. I wasn't even part of her care team. I never really had been. She was a check in the box to my school, and I had checked it. But I tried to pretend that she just didn't need me anymore. I did not convince myself.

And yet I learned to put it out of my mind. I've done it a thousand times since. And though it sounds grotesque, it's necessary. It took me a long time, but I created a switch in my brain. "You did all you could do."

Pushing Forward

Every rotation, I delved. There was the basic stuff, templates, algorithms, Task Force guidelines. Med school ticked on. The occasional conundrum or atypical presentation. That's what I loved. I was reminded time and again by my superiors that not everyone is a zebra. "When you see hoof prints, think horse not zebra." But I was still supposedly in remission despite all odds. I was an okapi. I always considered both the horses and zebras. I internalized all the times things didn't go as they were supposed to. It was both a source of hope and a cerebral exercise.

And then there were the times where medicine turned out to be the enemy, or where the system was exposed for its sacrifice of patients. I had no idea what to do with it. The reality of the harm of my noble career became unavoidable. I've never learned what to do with those tears. But they were necessary. In the years of COVID it has become all the more clear. The pain was indelible and inevitable and had to be survived. Reality as a survivor was overlapping all too well with the unwinnable fight of being a doctor. Nothing has made that more apparent than war.

I was training at Bethesda and Walter Reed in the 2007–2009 timeframe. I will never reconcile those horrors. It wasn't just the IED wounds. It was the heroism. It bore ungodly costs.

I will never forget the sound of that child wailing "that's not my daddy." She couldn't have been more than five. I was on a surgical rotation and more were being medevac'd every day. Her father wasn't even my patient. But after I witnessed what I saw, I asked about him. And I vomited later that night just sitting with it.

He had sustained head trauma in Afghanistan. He was in the common room in a helmet because they had to remove part of his skull and it wasn't time to put it back yet. He looked about my age. He was ranting and raving about all the things he wanted to 'fuck', cursing left and right, filled with an uncontainable rage that wasn't directed toward anyone or anything in particular. His speech was almost childlike. A young woman with young child in tow sat in a chair while he wandered around the room and her daughter wailed.

He shouldn't have lived. How could we do this to him and his family with the best efforts of medicine? How could this be their reality now? How could they stop it? He was no longer critical enough for cessation of care. He was stuck like this. Her father was stuck like this.

There were better days. There were different horrors that were far more positive. The Master Chief Corpsman who had been riddled with bullets. Half his colon, his gallbladder, his spleen, much of his abdominal wall, had been removed in Germany before he got to us. He was in the surgical ICU, talking, laughing. When I went to examine him and I lifted the sheet, I could see through him to the bed behind. He made it.

The woman who had not been a victim of war, but of life. She had a cardiac bypass. She went to skilled nursing and heard a strange crunching sound when she coughed. Once she sought care, they discovered an infection of her chest wall. After debridement and transfer to the ICU, I didn't have to listen to her chest to check her heartbeat. I could see her rhythm through the hole in her chest. And she made it, too.

What kind of sickening power was this? How do I and my colleagues reconcile it? It's seemingly inhuman. And you never know which way it's going to go.

There was one time in the midst of all that, where I knew that I couldn't control much, but I was sure as hell going to be able to live with what I could do. It was the same rotation as I witnessed the frontal lobe damaged father with the horrified child. A group of guys came through Germany to us. IEDs had taken a bunch of them out. The traumatic amputations were nearly uniform.

We were rounding one morning and a double amputee was having chest pain. We ordered an EKG and immediately sent him to the ICU. He was showering his lungs with clots after we took his mangled legs. Multiple heart attacks too. The same day we transferred him to the ICU, we got notice that the President, GW, was going to come to the ward for a photo op the next day. In preparation, we were ordered to transfer him back to the ward so that it could be a simple loop of the ward by the president as the media covered it.

I lost my mind. I went to the chief of surgery and told him that the patient's care was being compromised. He simply wasn't ready to go back to the ward. The chief assured me it wouldn't happen on his watch. I told him that if it did happen, I was going to need tomorrow off. I couldn't commit to being respectful to the commander-in-chief in this circumstance. He assured me it wouldn't be an issue. He told me later that day that I had tomorrow off.

My idealistic mind couldn't reconcile it. I had no choice, so I stayed away as I had said would be appropriate. Fast-forward to COVID times, and I'm grateful for the preparation that offered me for real life. A doctor's power is finite, and the system doesn't necessarily care what's right. There have been many times I have relearned that lesson. I won't go any farther into COVID here. That's its own journey. I had a whole different path to traverse first. A most welcome one.

Fourth Year

I was nearly through. Almost coasting. More electives in the last semester. But 2009 started out with a shot to the chest. A beloved friend died suddenly of a heart attack. I found out the following day. The news destroyed me. I could barely stand. I just kept collapsing on the floor, wailing. And the flight home for his funeral consisted of me putting my coat over my head to muffle the sobs. He had meant the world to me.

Knowing Joe and Elaine had transformed my concept of love and family. The adoration was constant and remarkable. It was what love should look like. And he, in particular, was just so ridiculous. We got up to many antics together. When he met my then husband, before even that, he ordered "a bottle of white and a bottle of red for each of us." He and I literally ended up sitting under the table at a nice restaurant, laughing raucously and drinking from the bottle by the end of the night. Just hysterical madness. He had been there after that 2005 surgery, showed up with straws in his nose declaring "I brought my own tubes!" I had prepared him for the many drains I may have.

I had gone through partial menopause after my surgery. Sweats like I couldn't believe, all sorts of vasomotor symptoms. There was clearly extensive damage to my spinal nerves. I was convinced I couldn't have kids after all that. And my neurosurgeon had told me my back wouldn't support a pregnancy anyway, but I had my goal, though long-term. Out of caution I stayed on birth control most of the time. And, it wasn't really much of an issue. Let's just say that most of my attention and focus was on med school.

But a rare occasion occurred on the day of Joe's death. I wouldn't find out about his passing until the next day. And as I was drinking wine in his kitchen mourning his death, I commented that I thought I would have a child soon, sipping my wine. I had zero knowledge that I was pregnant, but I just had a feeling the time was coming.

After getting back to San Diego and work for about a month, I was watching *Desperate Housewives* one afternoon. Eva Longoria was craving spicy foods and had breast tenderness. She was pregnant. I stopped for a moment to reconcile my own recent complaints and drove straight to the store for a pee stick. It was positive. I was 5 weeks. The only day it could have been was the day Joe died and before I knew. There is still a strong feeling that my daughter embodies Joe's best qualities, and I like to think some of his spirit made it there.

So I was a fourth-year med student with major back surgery and sequelae, not supposed to be able to have a kid, not even really supposed to be healthy and cancer-free, and at 5 weeks the pee stick was positive. I was beaming. I still am just for the privilege of growing that beautifully kind, intelligent, and powerful human being. There was no chance I would ever let her go. I emailed my neurosurgeon to let her know I was going forward and to ask for any specific guidance. There was none.

Pregnancy was godawful. Total bloodhound nose, which is particularly unpleasant when rotating through sports medicine. Five months of hyperemesis gravitarum, surviving on Fruit Loops and citrus. The nausea and vomiting was constant.

I lost more feeling in my legs going running at 22 weeks. That's when the running stopped. But I spent most of my seconds with my hand on my belly. I listened to her heartbeat with my stethoscope as I laid in bed trying to nap. She was my pride and joy from the second I knew her little clumps of cells were growing. Guts in my chest didn't feel great, but I was grateful.

My then husband was gone most of the pregnancy on deployment so I just worked and worked on growing her. She was everything, and I thought I had my life back. So many odds left behind. So many good things ahead. Who could stop me now?

So I made it through the rest of fourth year. I had graduated growing her. I was a doc. I had her a few months into internship. It was soul-crushing to have to send her to daycare after six weeks and move on with my training, but

I kept loving medicine and loving her when I got home. I made a little baby cage from a child gate, closing in an area in our living room. When I needed to pass out post-call when she was mobile, I would just lay down in there with some toys and just let her crawl over me while I rested. My life was complete, exhausting and complete.

We found a great nanny by her six-week mark and things were going beautifully. She was progressing normally, the cutest being I had ever encountered. She would get sick like any child and I would torment myself with the worst-case scenarios. And then I would suspend motherhood for a sec, engage doctor me, and realize that she was going to be okay.

It was going great…until the leg drag started again. She was just past her first birthday, and me finishing my internship, when all of a sudden, Mama couldn't walk or carry her anymore.

Just in Case

The day before my surgery in 2010, I knew things would get bad. I was pretty sure I would die. Casey was one year old. I sat down and wrote her bullet points to guide her though life without me.

Dear Casey,

I do not write this to shape you into my own mold, for your shape is your own and will continue to evolve by your hands and those around you. But I don't know how long I will be around, and I hope to share some of myself to spare you some of the tumult that comes as you discover and define who you are.

I adore you, Mom

FOR CASEY:

Things I want you to know, *JUST IN CASE:*

1. However bad things get, laughing or crying will usually make you feel at least a little bit better (especially if you're laughing at an inappropriate comment).

2. There's nothing like being kind to frustrate a jerk.

3. There is always a silver lining, it's just hard to find sometimes. Devoting energy to finding that lining rather than agonizing over what you cannot change often helps.

4. There are so many people that love you and would do anything for you, and it isn't just because our family and friends love me and want to help.

5. People do let you down sometimes. We are all weak jerks sometimes. The key is that you learn from the experience and look hard at yourself to figure out why you did it.

6. We all get lost. Figuring out who we are is a long and winding trek. Surviving pain is what gives us perspective and allows us to reach out and help others. Above all, try to reduce regret.

7. If it's inappropriate but clever, it's funny. If it's hateful, it's wrong. All hate stems from ignorance and fear.

8. A degree does not equal intelligence, but it does a hell of a lot to help you get by in the world. And, with few exceptions, it really doesn't matter what you get your degree in as long as you enjoy learning about it.

9. All you can do is your best. Stressing out about whether you will succeed just wastes energy you could apply to your goal. (I am a HUGE hypocrite, by the way!)

10. This is a big one. Every boy (or girl, whatever) you like will not like you. If you have to be anyone other

than yourself to win affections, everyone loses in the end.

11. Bad things happen. Sometimes they are so bad that we cannot fathom going on. The only thing that we can control is our own responses to the good and bad. The rest is out of our hands. A nap and/or hanging out with a good friend usually helps. Getting really drunk usually makes it worse: nausea + headache + sad = not helpful.

12. I'm sure it is no surprise to you at this point that mama used to be a lush. My dad taught me a very important lesson when I got out of control in college and was depressed and drinking too much. Alcohol is a food and a drug. If you ever get enveloped in your own need for it, you can't enjoy it anymore. And if you get to the point that you have to stop for your own emotional or physical health, you have lost out on a food that is so very diverse and complex that you will probably forever regret it.

13. Take care of your loved ones and be a kind stranger, but beware of people that have a need for drama and avoid those that always call but never pick up the phone.

14. There is never any excuse for hurting animals or children. People that take advantage of the weak and vulnerable are to be feared. They have no conscience.

15. Ideally, we hurt no one, but we must defend ourselves or those that depend on us for safety. It can probably be done with words. Try.

16. You can have a small amount of the richest foods anytime, as long as you are willing to do 5–10 minutes of abdominal exercises 5 days a week. A large amount of rich foods is a waste. Their novelty is the draw (and heavy foods make you feel like crap after a while).

17. You have a responsibility to yourself and those in your care to be moderate in your vices.

18. Pain, fever, and weight are harder to get rid of than prevent, but if they occur, it takes dedication and compliance with an organized health plan to get rid of.

19. People that love you appreciate your willingness to ask for help. It makes their job easier.

20. Always tip well. Share, especially the good stuff.

21. Find a way to love yourself, even when you are at your worst.

22. When you don't know what to do, tell your story to yourself. It will help you organize your thoughts and figure out where the decisions really lie. Be strong but caring in your response and pick the path that gets the suffering over with and leads to better things.

23. You can validate people's concerns without giving them what they want OR ask for.

24. When you tell people things that make them sad or mad, make sure you are clear on your own intentions.

25. There is not a person in the world, young or old, that you cannot stand to learn from and share your own knowledge with; the lesson that you learn from

them may not always be the one they are trying to teach you, though.

26. Know that I have never loved as I do you. Dream of me. I will be there.

Three hours with tears running down my cheeks in a restaurant. Finding the words to say goodbye. Finding a way to leave some part of me with the love of my life as my gut wrenched with fear of what was to come.

And then time to go home, hold her, and look at the face that would change by the time I got back. If I got to come back.

Counting Tiles

Over the course of a year, my life dissolved in front of me. I was becoming paralyzed from the scar tissue. We would try to debride it, to open the cysts, to decrease the pressure on my nerves. Long and short, we failed. A surgery that was intended to save my legs led to three years of ICU stays, dire predictions, and the total collapse of who I thought I was. And to the total collapse of who everyone else thought I was.

Surgery went fine. Or so we thought. I was in the hospital for a few weeks. We had ripped my back open, again, and tried to release the adhesions on my spinal nerves. Weeks without my baby. Lying in a hospital bed. Worthy work so I could be a fully functional mama again. The pain was out of this world, but the physical pain was nothing comparatively. The slightest movement was agony, but it was nothing. Absolutely nothing compared to what the next few years would bring.

I was passing time. I was putting in the work. I would get better, walk, return to my life, my motherhood, my career, whatever else there was to my life. It was just a matter of time. And Thanksgiving was coming. I wanted to be home for the holiday. Scrubs giving with my friends and family. Let me go home.

A few days before Thanksgiving, I had a fever to 103 in the middle of the night. The nurse said it was atelectasis, or bogginess of the lungs due to inactivity. I asked him to call the intern or resident to order blood cultures. He refused. "You're a patient, not a doctor right now." I went back to sleep.

I think I got out on a Tuesday. There wasn't much time before Thanksgiving. My friend had rented a house at the beach for our holiday and me, my daughter, and my then husband went. I couldn't really eat. I spent much of the time curled up on the floor, shaking in a blanket. I got up and played with my daughter, took a couple pictures of us in our scrubs and her adorable baby scrubs. She laid with me for a bit as I curled back up on the floor. I knew I was febrile. But I just needed her for a minute. And she needed me.

We went home the next day. My head felt like it was going to pop. I already knew the answer. It was incalculable pain. I was shivering and sweating. I looked like death. And for good reason.

We got back to the condo. I jumped in the shower. I bawled from the pain and knowledge of what was happening. I obviously had meningitis. Recent back surgery, a headache that cannot be described. I checked my blood pressure. Dangerously low. Yep.

"You're going to have to drop me off at the ER."

"What do you mean?"

"Drop me off. They're going to admit me."

A look of confusion from my then husband.

I said goodbye to my daughter again. It was crippling. I thought I had escaped it, the gnawing feeling before my last surgery that I wouldn't watch my daughter grow up. The note I wrote her telling her how much I love her and simple lessons I had learned from life in case I wasn't there. All those nights lying in bed thinking I had escaped the demise I felt so near. And here we were.

I went to the check-in desk, trying to contain my pain and fear.

"I just had a back surgery and now I have an uncontrollable headache and low blood pressure. I'm septic."

"Have a seat."

The tears were uncontrollable. I was sobbing.

The charge nurse was dipping behind the desk for a snack (they kept the candy and chips there).

"That's doc. She doesn't cry. Get her back."

Within minutes, I was on a cot. Morphine wasn't far behind. Immediate MRI. I gathered my gown across my bare ass to go to the center of the ER to log in to see the image. Not good.

There was a large abscess. Huge. Epidural. Neurosurgery was en route. This was it.

Weeks more counting ceiling tiles in the hospital. They had tried to cut out the infection. It was in my CSF. IV antibiotics. Months of them. And years of complications ahead. The infection had undone anything that we had tried to do. It wasn't just my legs at risk anymore, it was my life. And we were far from done.

The Undoing

I've thought a lot about how to engage this part of my life honestly. I don't know that I can. I effectively ceased to be myself. I lost everything, or so I thought. All at once, every aspect of my self-definition crumbled. I tried to survive, to protect my life and my daughter. It didn't seem like I succeeded, but eventuality has been kind. By no means was it secure.

They had to reconstruct my back. My surgeon told me that he had never done anything like it before. "I just kept cutting out tissue and then rolling and sewing and gluing to try to create a semblance of a back. You have no tissue planes."

So, I pretty much had to learn to walk yet again. I had a PICC line (an IV in my upper arm that delivered antibiotics close to my heart and could stay in up to eight weeks). I was on convalescent leave again. A nurse came to my house to tend to me. I had a backpack with a constant infusion of antibiotics. It rested on my pillow when I tried to sleep. I had to keep my one-year-old from pulling on it. I couldn't lift anything. I couldn't lift her.

I tried to keep being a mom. She was and is my everything. But I was limited. I couldn't be a doctor. My job was to survive. I didn't even really want to be a wife. It was very unclear as to whether I had a future. The pain was constant.

As time went on, I was supposed to get back to work, to training. Another MRI, this time by Infectious Diseases. I went from the imaging suite to my office. I read it myself. And, shit. Huge abscess. This time higher up and next to my thoracic spine. I went straight to the chief resident. He pulled it up. "Let's wait for the read." There was a 7×1.5cm hole in my back. Likely infected.

More IV antibiotics. More nausea. More weight loss. More pain. Eventually, I went back to work, often in a wheelchair, with PICC line in. I did my Infectious Diseases rotation with a life-threatening infection. My supervisors were my docs. They wanted to watch me if I was going to come back.

As much as I loved being back in it, the answer was clear. I wasn't ready. The pain was terrible. The risk was high. It was obviously unwise. But docs do stupid things for themselves while they tell others not to. We sacrifice our very selves to the hours and the fatigue while cautioning others not to. This embodied that. After that month, I acknowledged I couldn't do it. I took a research month and wrote an Infectious Diseases paper with the help and guidance of a colleague and mentor. More time.

UCSF

I got a consult to UCSF Neurosurgery. We had made things worse by operating. My legs were still failing and now I was fighting a life-threatening infection. Somebody must be able to help me. Someone must be able to save my legs.

We flew to San Francisco, my then husband and I. I was an interesting case. Surely someone could debride the scar tissue around my tangled nerves without killing me. My life as I knew it couldn't be gone. Someday I would pick my daughter up again, round the wards without wheels. Please, God, help me.

So we made an appointment. Showed up. Waited, as per the norm. After what seemed like forever, a middle-aged man with a watch that cost more than my car walked in. Let's just say we didn't exactly have rapport.

"I might be able to help, but if I operate then you are mine. I'll own you."

Not going to try to remember my response, but it was as polite as humanly possible, "I'm sorry?"

He went on to tell me that if he put scalpel to skin, I would have to stay there. No one else could touch me. I was his. Unfortunately, this was not the last time I would hear this.

"I'm in the Navy, stationed in San Diego. I have a daughter. I can't stay."

I don't even know what he said after that. It wasn't good. I stepped outside to call my neurosurgeon's cell. "Kat, stop looking for a scalpel. You won't make it. I'll keep doing what I can."

So we went home. I had walked in with hope and met a man who neither regarded me as a human nor a doctor. I had become accustomed to sexism as a female Navy doc, but this male doctor told his colleague, a woman, that the only path forward was to submit and submit with absolute degradation. It didn't exactly seem like a good plan.

More and more it seemed like there wasn't a place to go. In my mind, the wheels became my inevitability. My future as a doctor and a mother all the more convoluted, if even possible.

Trying

I was broken. There was very little I could do, and that was on a good day. The months were weighing heavy. The prognosis seemed to be getting worse. And then I couldn't eat. Infection? Meds? A return of the cancer? We didn't know. But we knew I was wasting away.

My then husband couldn't take it anymore. I was often in a wheelchair. I couldn't chase my toddler. Any given day was unpredictable. So he requested a billet to Africa. I had already referred to him as my 'roommate' to my mentor. The walls were closing in. Due to my debility, my docs didn't let him go to Africa. I couldn't do it without him. And not long after, I left him. But not yet.

I was back on outpatient. I had to show up for morning report. My feet were flopping. I crossed paths with the chief resident on the way. I was moving more slowly than usual. He was walking with one of the staff. As I tried to get my legs to do what I wanted, my commands weren't heard. I could hear my feet slapping the ground. I saw their faces as they watched my gait as I approached. Within days, my legs stopped working altogether. I couldn't feel below my waist.

It was time for a shunt. We had to relieve the pressure on my nerves.

My then husband wanted to go visit a friend. It was all too much. My surgery was scheduled for midweek. His flight was Friday. When he booked it, we didn't know if I would still be paralyzed that weekend, chasing our toddler. I told him it was okay to go. I meant it. By the time he returned, I was done.

Nothing had made it more clear to me that whatever time I had left wouldn't be spent like this. But leaving him didn't stop my physical spiral, and not being able to take care of my daughter on my own started a far more severe emotional one.

Brief Respite

For just a minute, I thought I might be past it all. My shunt worked. Sensation and function restored. I went home. I was walking, no flopping of feet. Another reprieve. I was scared of the foreign body securing my legs' function, but I had hope again. I could do it.

I returned to work. Back on my feet, no wheels. Rushing around and doing my job. Fear abated. Life was coming back online. I didn't even go to my follow-up with my neurosurgeon. I was too busy working, back to saving lives, facing challenges, helping people. That being said, my confidence that I would live or keep walking was gone. I didn't know how long I would even be able to feel below my waist.

I had a pouch on my back where the shunt crossed over my spinal column and around to my abdomen. Small price to pay. I was back and I could live. My marriage had been exposed in my mind as useless, but I could work and mother again. I left and considered new prospects. I had a future after all. I was still recovering, but I might be able to take care of Casey again. I might be able to pick her up again.

Hope. No confidence, just hope. And it varied by the minute.

I moved in with a friend. She even made Casey a room in her house. I was back to life and trying to race toward happiness with my renewed legs. I was still broken by the last year, unsure of my future, but it seemed I had one. Maybe.

I had already started looking at romantic alternatives. Physical pleasure, though momentary, was one of the few things that I still knew I had, at least after the shunt. Everything else was still tenuous. The concept of someone new understanding my plight was another lifesaver. Early on in relationships, you aren't an inconvenience. You can limit how much of your pain they see. You can almost choose who they can see.

I had boyfriends immediately. One very complicated, one blissfully simple. Each aware of the other. Each nonexclusive. The escape was there, as were new trials.

A friend of years, gorgeous, funny, and kind, appeared. My 33rd birthday and we spent it together. The complicated boyfriend awkwardly stopped by. We all sat for a bit before Cam and I went to play some pool. The complicated boyfriend was on his way to a date. Cam and I talked and laughed and he didn't seem disturbed by the weird pouch in my back when I showed him. Not long after, it was clear there was mutual attraction.

It was a strange time. It was my divorce year and I played. It was sometimes complicated, sometimes simple. I hadn't dated for over a decade. The complicated one receded, but we worked together, so there were setbacks. Cam and I made it clear to each other that there were no strings.

And then, one day, on a rotation with the complicated on-and-off boyfriend, my legs started to fail. I had to leave the ward and pass off the pager to head to my neurosurgeon.

"Hot Damn"

I walked down the hallway the back way, poked my head in the door, and he saw me. We talked about how I had been, reveled in his success with the shunt, and considered what to do next, what was going on. Why were they failing again? We had made so much progress. There must be a simple solution.

He was proud of me for being back at work. We figured we had weathered the worst. We had developed a friendly rapport based on his track record of saving my life and legs. We caught up.

He blushed and asked me if I remembered post-op after the shunt. I said I did not. I told him I had asked the anesthesiologist to go easy on me, noting that my colleagues were operating on me and caring for me, and that I would rather be in pain than embarrass myself to them. The anesthesiologist did not heed my request.

"Kat, it was the funniest thing I've ever seen."
"What? What did I do?"
"In post-op."

"Oh, God."

His face was beet red and he was chuckling. I knew it was good. I told them to go easy on the anesthesia! Head in my hands.

"I would have videoed it if it wouldn't have cost me my career."

"Ugh, just tell me."

"I came to check on you in post-op and asked you if you could feel your legs." Face got more red, more chuckling.

"What did I do?" (with urgency)

"You said, 'lemme see'."

"And…"

"And you lifted up the sheet, reached down with your hand, and said, 'Hot damn! I can feel my hooha!' I almost fell down laughing."

I couldn't help but laugh my ass off. It was a good one. Ugh. Stupid anesthesia.

A momentary laugh. Finding the positives in the road. Surely there was something we could do here. Another way forward.

So, it was time to deal with the current situation. What are we going to do next? What do we need to fix? We talked about my legs failing, he did a neuro exam, and he furrowed his brow. I mentioned the pouch on my back since the shunt was placed, verifying that it was normal. Another furrowing of his brow and the lifting of the back of my shirt. All blood drained from his face.

"Well, that's an F-ing interesting physical finding, Kat! Damn it!"

"I thought it was normal. It's been there since the surgery. I tried looking it up and couldn't find pics of what a lumboperitoneal shunt is supposed to look like."

A growl. "Surgery tomorrow."

Another abscess. Back to the depths. On to my second shunt and ripping my back open again.

Shunt #2

Back in pre-op. My third major back surgery in a year. Paralysis back on the table. More infection. More leave from residency. More time not holding Casey. More fear that I wouldn't see her grow up. Desperately trying to hold on to hope.

The complicated boyfriend was on a rotation just down the hall. Me in a cot awaiting surgery. No hand on mine. And then a text from Cam trying to figure out how to get to me. He came to sit with me. A smile by my side. A hand to hold. Just knowing he still doesn't care about my existing disfigurement and that to come. Not being alone in my fear.

Rescue

Discharged to staying with my friend. More antibiotics, and antifungals this time too. Staph and Candida. And with all the meds, the inability to eat seemed to be getting worse. I kept shrinking.

By now, my friend did the lion's share of taking care of my daughter when I had her. Casey was almost two and could walk and crawl faster than I could. I was on a host of meds. I wasn't sure I'd wake up if she needed me. I was useless again.

She was the classic child who kicks when she sleeps. She would drive herself in circles through the night. When we snuggled, the kicks would land squarely on my wound. I screamed into the pillow and just held it tight. It wasn't her fault. She was just a toddler and her mother was broken. And the broken wasn't going away.

My neurosurgeon told me, "You have to sit. Do nothing. I don't want you to move or you might die. You just won't heal."

For all I had achieved, all I had, I couldn't do any of it or I might die. I wasn't a mom anymore, not safely. I wasn't a doc. I had willingly given up wife status. I knew that I had to survive. But I didn't know what merely surviving meant. I didn't know if there was any of me actually left. I had to face that I couldn't take care of her.

My ability to mother was seemingly gone. I didn't know which moments my legs would function, which moments the pain would allow me to get out of bed, when I was going to be incapacitated by which med, whether I would be heaving over a toilet or trash can at any moment. I was nothing. I had to accept it. There's no way I would let her get hurt on my watch. It took me years of therapy to unlearn that I was 'a piece of shit'.

Just in Case...

As I sat wrestling with the likelihood of my death again in fall 2011, and as I writhed emotionally at the distance from my daughter, I figured I might as well expound on those bullet points that I wrote when predicting my own death in 2010.

1. However bad things get, laughing or crying will usually make you feel at least a little bit better (especially if you're laughing at an inappropriate comment).

When I was diagnosed with my cancer back in 2005, the neurosurgeons couldn't believe that I walked into the office to get my MRI results. The cancer should have paralyzed me long before it was detected. The surgery to remove it had an estimated 100% chance of lower extremity paralysis given that the tumor was wrapped around the nerves to my legs, not to mention those to my bowel and bladder.

Needless to say, I was terrified of what was going to happen to me and my legs. But, no matter what I did, the risks were going to stay the same. I had the president's neurosurgeon operating on me at Bethesda, and by the time I got home from the hospital, your dad's boss had gotten the letter faxed from my surgeon saying that he was going to need some time off to take care of me. Not only that, but they extended your dad in the Navy that day. He was originally supposed to get out a few months later, but my diagnosis turned our world around, so we needed to make sure we were financially secure, no matter what happened.

Our financial concerns were ameliorated, I had the best doctors working on me, and the rest was left to chance. Well, most of the rest. I could still control how I was going to spend the next six days, possibly my last on two feet. So I went dancing, and I joked with my friends about how 'tricked out' my wheelchair would be. Joe and Elaine and I drank wine and tried to come up with tasteless jokes that would keep us laughing instead of crying.

I did cry, of course, but not all that much. The tears didn't make me feel any better and didn't change what the outcome was going to be. I would have cried constantly, would still be crying, if it made any difference, but so would everyone else. The world would run on tears if that was true.

But, laughter is different. It actually makes you feel better. It starts a positive feedback loop that builds on itself. It reminds you that you still have some power. You can choose to laugh, and no matter how bad the joke, or how painful the truth behind the joke is, that laughter reminds you that things could be worse. They can always be worse.

2. There's nothing like being kind to frustrate a jerk.

People who are being mean are usually doing so because someone was mean to them and they are projecting it outward. They may not even be conscious of how cruel they are acting, but feel wronged in some way, and being obnoxious to others is somehow supposed to make them feel better, feel bigger. They may not even know that it isn't 'normal' to put others down. But the reality is that being mean makes you smaller. It proves that you think so little of yourself that you have to step on someone else to feel significant, to feel like you matter. All that you prove is that you are insecure.

This is most dangerous in childhood and adolescence. Nothing quite makes sense, or made sense to me, at that age. The vulnerability of changing bodies, fluctuating neurotransmitters, and feeling alienated from your family and friends while simultaneously seeking approval from them is both exhausting and frustrating.

I was miserable and confused. When I was in middle school I wanted so much to belong to the cliques—which usually maintained leaders but traded followers on a weekly basis—that I even made fun of my best friend at one point to seek acceptance. I know 'best friend' is a term that gets used a lot, but I'm talking about Ave, who by now you know quite well.

At the risk of telling a story you've heard a million times by now, we were friends from the second we met. In fourth grade, I visited Maret, and it happened to be on the day of a field trip. I walked into the classroom of the lower school, was introduced, and immediately was either beckoned or walked over to Ave, and we have been best friends ever since. Family, really, with only a couple rifts in the twenty-some years since then.

Now, that is not to say that we did not make fun of each other, even from that very first day. It's is important to know the difference between a friendly joke that allows us to laugh at ourselves and each other, and a mean-spirited comment or action. When we were on the bus for the field trip the first day I met Ave, I fell asleep against the window in the back of the bus as I tried to fight off my carsickness. 'Fire! Fire!' Ave had crept up to me as I slept and startled me awake. I jumped up and looked around crazily. Everyone around me laughed. But most importantly, I laughed, and Avery laughed with me. It's still funny even now, actually. I wish I could have seen my face.

I went to Maret after fourth grade because I was being bullied at my prior Elementary school, and I was miserable. That, and DC public schools were pretty bad then, so my parents made a lot of sacrifices so I could have a good education. All in all, I was very happy to go to Maret, and made some incredible friends there. They are still most of my closest friends. But, I fell into the adolescent trap of throwing my true friend under the bus to gain acceptance by others at one point. Despite the fact that was when I was eleven, I still feel badly about it.

But what feels awesome is watching the wince in someone else's eyes when they make some rude comment to you and you shrug it off and move on, proving it inconsequential. It makes them feel even lower than when they started, and it shows that they are wasting their time when trying to mess with you. Even better, you can ask them if you offended them in some way, and put them on the defense while also being more constructive. It's a win-win.

If someone threatens you physically, however, it is another story. There is part of me that wants to say "Kick their ass, or call me to do it for you," but that is ridiculous. People that are willing to fight physically when it is not unavoidable—or in the preservation of life or limb—can't be trusted not to fight dirty, and there is nothing casual or funny about trauma. Really bad things can happen easier than most people realize when violence is involved.

Luckily, I'm quite sure that your dad will make sure that you can fight, but only to defend yourself, and in a way that takes the person down quickly so that you can get the hell out of the situation, not take revenge. If a gun is ever involved, though, you only shoot if you are going to shoot to kill, otherwise you don't even point the gun near a person. And you only point it if there is no other option. Dad will teach you how to shoot, not because taking the life of any living thing is cool or even acceptable unless it's for survival, but because guns kill when people don't know how to use them. Plus, if a gun makes its way into your hand in a life or death situation, you better know what to do.

71

Sorry to harp on all of this, but knowing that you will be under emotional or physical distress and I may not be there to protect you gets me a little spun up. Just be careful. Be cautious and have the tools that you will need to face any situation, and you will be okay. That's all you can do.

3. There is always a silver lining, it's just hard to find sometimes. Devoting energy to finding that lining rather than agonizing over what you cannot change often helps.

My diagnosis in 2005 was devastating. Not only did I have my back split in two and bone sawed away, but the illusion of immortality was taken from me. Everything I thought I knew about my future was called into question. The potential loss of my legs, knowing that the cancer would most likely come back someday, and the likelihood that I would never be able to have children all sent my mind spinning. The physical pain was indescribable, but was dwarfed by the emotional pain and grief. But the self-discovery exceeded both, and today I am a much better doctor than I ever could have dreamed of being if I hadn't suffered illness and survived.

I often see people at their most terrified and devastated. Giving people diagnoses of fatal conditions is an unfortunate part of my job. But because of what I have been through, I can speak from experience and help people find the strength to get through the shock and muster the strength to deal with the news. The strength is theirs and I have only a minor role, but I have had many patients tell me what a difference it made to hear the perspective of a survivor. Illness is extremely isolating, and feeling like you have people around you that have been through similar experiences helps to alleviate the horror a little.

Every time I hear from one of my patients that my perspective has helped them get through the first days of their diagnosis, or see their families' faces regain a little color after I sit with them and explain the nature of the disease and the emotional beast that is upon them, I feel relief from my own burden. Somehow, even though my words likely make my patients' and their families' fears even more concrete, having some sense of understanding what is going on, and some validation of their plight makes it more tolerable. And seeing their relief does that same thing for me.

I have even had the recurrent ridiculous thought that maybe my cancer was a good thing. After all, it has certainly made me a better and more selfless person, and certainly happier due to newfound perspective. The thought is of course still obscenely ridiculous. I am making the best of the positives that have come from a horrible diagnosis that has set in motion a series of events that culminates in the very reason that I am writing this to you, the inevitability and potential immediacy of my own death.

It was a lot easier to rationalize my tumult before you came along. I always wanted kids and knew that I would love it, but I never knew that your smile would touch my soul. I know it has probably been said by many and sounds trite, but watching you smile and learn and laugh and play makes me want to cling to this Earth more than I ever wanted to before. Knowing that my absence will cause you pain makes me loathe my diagnosis all the more. It makes any thought of worthwhile purpose to the injustice of my illness laughable. But I have to remember how I came to be the person that is your mom.

Finding the silver lining has become a forte of mine, largely out of necessity given my saga of unfortunate medical events. But it is a strength that I cherish nonetheless. Good can always come from bad. You just have to find the good, refuse to let the bad win. With tragedy comes loss. The pain is there. There is nothing we can do to undo it. But we can shape what comes from it. We can refuse to let it own us, and cherish the joys that made that loss so unbearable.

One such loss for me was losing Joe. He was an odd combination of wonderful friend and father figure for me, and a man that was filled with brightness. He was not only incredibly smart, but kind, goodwilled, goodhearted, and ridiculously fun. I love him beyond measure and still feel the devastation of his loss. I still, more than two years after his death, break down crying while driving sometimes. But, though the world is a worse place without him, it is a far better place than it would have been if he had never been in it. His loss is only so great because of all of the wonderful times I shared with him.

Watching him and Elaine raise Anna and Duncan was inspirational. They were such incredibly loving parents and respected their kids as individuals as long as I have known them. Anna's purple hair was not a betrayal of them, but an expression of herself. Duncan's track meets hours away were privileges to attend for them, never cursed obligations. It was refreshing. And watching Joe and Elaine together was what love stories try to capture. Their mutual love, respect, and trust seeped from every pore when they looked at each other.

I cannot imagine the loss that Joe's family feels now that he is no longer physically here, but I know that I would not trade my pain for anything in this world. I got to know him, and for that I will gladly pay whatever price is asked of me. More than that, I still have Elaine, Dunk, and Anna, not to mention all of the other wonderful friends and family in my life. Life is unpredictable, so I do my best to cherish those I love while I am still here and be thankful for the opportunity.

We all inevitably suffer loss in our lives. All we can do is learn to cope with the pain or be consumed by it. I was relieved to find that there is more joy to be gained from using my own pain to lessen that of others than I had realized. I will always savor the sweet despair of having known Joe. And though my time may well end before I would like, I got to make you, Casey, and for that I could not be more proud or grateful.

If you are reading this because I am gone, I am truly sorry. I cannot imagine the loss you will feel in not getting to grow up with a mother. I hope that this at least provides you with some sense of who I was and how much I love you. And I hope that you can take that loss and apply it to a constructive purpose. I think it will give you a great deal of relief and will make some sense of the injustice of my absence.

4. There are so many people that love you and would do anything for you, and it isn't just because our family and friends love me and want to help.

You have had a spark since the day you were born, and people are inevitably drawn to it. You originated on the day that Joe passed away (as I mentioned, I found out the next morning). I can't help but see some of his impish kindness in your eyes, even if it's just because he did such a good job nourishing it in me. I prefer to think that his spirit made its way to you in some way, though. You and he share this amazing positivity that brightens the world around you without being false.

Regardless of the parts of me, your dad, and all of those that have influenced us along the way that shine forth through you, you are purely you. Never let anyone else take ownership of you or your actions. No one else can determine who or what you should be, and any efforts to let others decide (or to defy them) will only start you on an inherently conflicting path. That being said, not everything you do has to be profound or launching you on some

76

important journey. Sometimes it is painfully unclear which path to take, or even where the paths lie. When that happens, just stop and think about what you truly enjoy and brainstorm about associated opportunities.

For instance, you already adore animals. A dog passes by, or appears on the TV screen, and nothing else matters. You smile, yell, point, and do everything within your power to make your way closer. So, say money is really tight at some point and you decide that you need to make some cash. Think about working at a pet shop, or a veterinarian's, or a dog wash. You may well find that there are things about it that you don't like, but figuring out which paths you do not want to take is often just as constructive as figuring out which ones you are interested in.

Life is largely a process of elimination. But remember that, you are not going to enjoy yourself all the time. Life is hard work, and therefore anything that we do in it will also require dedication, and usually entail some hardship. The question is, do you net happiness from the experience, and how low do the worst experiences take you? If the worst is tolerable and you gain more happiness than you spend energy laboring over the endeavor, then you are in a good place. If not, take stock of the skills and lessons that you have learned from the experience, and make preparations to move on. Sometimes this means looking for another type of job in the same field, the same job at a different location, or going back to brainstorming about what makes you happy and applying what you have learned to something else entirely. Whatever happens, you have gained the wisdom of experience and perseverance in the process.

Most importantly, though, do not worry about what other people want from you (until you start a family and become a team that has to work together toward common goals). What you do with your life is your decision, and as long as you are realistic about what the demands, sacrifices, and benefits will be, then you cannot go wrong. Along those lines, though, you do NEED a good education. Life becomes very difficult when employers don't have clear evidence that you can apply yourself to a goal and succeed. It is up to you to decide what it is that drives you, interests you, and where you want to carve out your niche, but that can only be done with a lot of dedication to learning AND obtaining credentials that prove it to those judging you for employment.

Who you are inside, and what you apply your energies to, are entirely up to you. Those that love you will be there to support you along the way. Unfortunately, no matter what you decide about those things, you will still need money. You may not need a lot of money. That is also up to you. You decide what things you need, how much space you really want, and how much travel (or other similarly expensive opportunities) matter to you. Once you determine that, then you can decide how it is you will get there. This usually means more schooling, internships, or other forms of training/education. Just remember, that though these things are demanding and may sap you of time and energy, they will provide you with the knowledge that allows you opportunity in the future.

There are more things than money that provide opportunity, including the people that you know and whether or not you have been willing to help them in the past, but money is the most powerful form of opportunity in this world, at least as it is now. Money allows you to help people, and yourself, when times get difficult, and that makes a huge difference when it comes to quality of life.

More than anything, I want you to have a happy and rewarding life filled with love. Those things are far more important than money will ever be. I just want to make sure you consider all of these things as you are deciding who you want to be in your life. Ease is a wonderful thing. It makes everything else all the more enjoyable, and money frequently, but not always, equals greater ease as long as you remember that love and kindness are never to be sacrificed in the name of money.

Number four was as far as I got at that time. Trying to survive was a full-time job. And finding a place in my brain that was centered and eloquent was only an occasional occurrence.

Segue

I'm going to take a moment. I've thought about writing a thousand times. I've had many friends and acquaintances encourage me to tell my story. But it felt either self-justifying in my misery or just vain, self-serving. I didn't see the point other than to self-coddle. Why would anyone want to hear my story?

But there is a reason. It is a greater effort than anything that has to do with me, even remotely. Survival. Perseverance. The value of the fight, depths and all.

I have been people I despise. Though I may never forgive them, I can live with them. But only because I will not repeat them. I think that echoes in many people's lives, cancer or no. Life-threatening illness or no. Cataclysmic collapse of self or no.

There is part of me that wants to almost excuse the people I have been. But I cannot do that in good conscience. Have I built on my pain? Yes. Have I acknowledged it and inwardly atoned, yes. But it will not go away. I don't get to do that. I live with it and build from it. We all have the bottom in us, we just hope we never get there. And when we do, we need to find a way back to the surface.

Summary

From 2010 to 2012, I withstood horrors. Shunt, abscess, legs failing. Next shunt, fistula. Leaking CSF from my skin when I stood up was particularly terrifying. A freaking durocutaneous fistula. A channel of skin that formed by scar from my spinal column to the outside world. I've never even read about it. And when I tried to seek help, my Infectious Diseases doc immediately sent me to neurosurgery. The physician assistant on call said I was fine. But every time I stood up or changed positions, the fluid circulating around my brain and spinal cord would leak out through a hole in my back. I could die of a fatal infection incredibly easily. I left a message for my neurosurgeon on his cell.

"Kat, I just got your message. I can't even go skiing. You try to die every time. Go to the hospital. I'll operate in the morning."

"Can I just go at 04:30? I won't eat after midnight."

"God damn it, Kat. Go."

"Yes, sir."

That led to my third shunt. All he could do was remove the second shunt, push glue into the hole, and find the one remaining spot for my third shunt. My back was a mess. But that wasn't the end of it. The third shunt over-drained. The headaches started. I had to cover one eye to read or look at a computer. The pain being upright was indescribable. We didn't know the mechanism yet.

I only made it a couple months of that kind of progressive pain before I hung up my hat in residency.

"I haven't killed anyone yet, I'm not going to start now. I'll die or kill someone if I keep trying." I went from the top of my residency class, being told "you're one of the three best on the wards, even with your illness"...to "you're ruining your life and you won't be able to provide for your daughter" in three days. February 2012. I said I couldn't do it anymore. And I was immediately blackballed. Doctors aren't allowed to be that sick.

I ran into my neurosurgeon in the courtyard after I withdrew. He could barely look at me.

"I worked so hard to get you through."
"I know, sir. I'm sorry. But I'll die if I keep pushing. I can't do it."

He looked down, saddened and angry. He rushed off to wherever he was supposed to be.

He had saved my life. Over and over. He had laughed with me, probably wanted to cry with me. He had cared. And I had let him down. But I had to push on and push through, and I simply couldn't do that with the rigor of residency. I was back to the job of surviving. And he was still there to support me.

Crushing head pain. Consults. Mayo. A UTI that almost killed me. A C2 tap that was dry. No CSF to pull out. A valve on my shunt.

Mayo

I didn't have much left. Death was constantly rattling around me. There was no moving on, no matter how desperately I tried. Somebody must be able to help me.

So I made my way to Mayo Clinic. Neurosurgery again. Wasn't there something, somewhere, that could save my legs and my life? Wasn't there some way I could get my daughter, the child I was never supposed to be able to have, back?

I put together a synopsis of my horrific past. My rare cancer, the complications that should have killed me, the MRI of a paralyzed or dead person. Surely I was interesting enough to help. And it seemed I was.

I got there. A hotel room. Plans for a C2 tap (drawing out fluid from my cervical spine just beneath the base of my brain), exceptionally dangerous, to figure out the status of my CSF. At that level, it's easy to puncture the brain stem, potentially fatal or devastating. We had a date planned. And an appointment with neurosurgery. Someone was going to figure me out.

But as I waited in the hotel room, wandering the small surrounding town, I started to feel sick. Pain peeing. A slight fever that picked up steam. Shaking in bed. A total loss of time.

My tap was supposed to be the next day, but I lay shaking in bed. I called the very kind and understanding man who was coordinating my care because he felt for the devastating, and intriguing, set of events I had withstood.

"I don't think they should do the stick. I'm ill."

"What's going on?"

"I have a fever and I can't stop shaking. I might be septic."

He picked me up. I sat rigoring, curled up on a bench in front of the hotel awaiting him. I was dry heaving and drenched in sweat. He took me to the ER immediately.

When I got there, my heart rate was 160ish. My blood pressure dangerously low. I offered my diagnosis at intake, "UTI sepsis."

They immediately started fluids and IV antibiotics. They gathered blood and urine.

"Would you mind checking my kidney function and myoglobin?"

I told him I had been shaking for days and probably had rhabdomyolysis (damage to the kidneys caused by a muscle breakdown product that can occur when you shake uncontrollably). The resident smiled. I shared my history of internal medicine residency, rare cancer, near fatal complications, and the reason for my visit. The physician staff came by. They asked me, without condescension, if there was anything they were missing and anything else they should order.

"When you go back to residency, you should do it here."

"I'm not going back."

"Why not?"

"I'll die. Or I'll be paralyzed. My body can't take it. I'm just working on living and walking at this point." It hurt to say it again.

Even as I lay there, dangerously ill, the very people who were treating me wanted me to head down that dangerous path that had nearly killed me for two years now. I was resolute. I couldn't finish residency. But, ironically, I wouldn't have survived my hospital stay if I hadn't been a doctor.

The ICU

Initially, they sent me to the ward. My blood pressure was coming up with fluids and they were doing the needed tests. I seemed stable. My cognition was clearly intact.

At about 4am, they checked my vitals. Blood pressure 80 over palp. Dangerously low.

"Don't RRT me. I'm fine."

"We have to. You're critical."

"Just put my head down. Gimme a sec. Recheck in a minute, I'll try to bring my blood pressure up."

"Sorry, you know how this works."

It was just short of calling a Code Blue. I was at risk of dying, and immediately.

And off they carted me to the ICU. It was my fifth time in two years. At least it wasn't my colleagues putting in lines or catheters or doing hygiene this time. They turned up the fluids.

By the next morning, I looked like a marshmallow. It's called anasarca. My hospital bracelet was cutting into my wrist. I could only speak a word or two at a time between breaths. The team came in to see me: Staff, Fellow, Resident, Intern.

"You need a central line, an arterial line, and more fluids."

"No central line. You're not putting a line near my heart with bacteria in my blood. I don't want to risk endocarditis."

A shrug off. "Your blood pressure is dangerously low, you need more fluids. Are you in medicine?"

"I'm a doc. What I need is less fluids and Lasix. I have fulminant pulmonary edema."

"You don't have pulmonary edema. We would have heard it when we listened to your lungs."

"Yes"…gasp… "you would have"…gasp… "if any of you had listened to my lungs."

A look of shock on the staff's face as he looked around at his team. He abruptly walked out of the room and his team followed.

The intern came back in moments later and said, "You're right. And you're not in the Navy here. You can do what you want."

"No central or a-lines. No more fluids. Turn them off. Get me some Lasix." Many gasps in between.

She smiled and left.

I didn't want to risk an infection of my heart valves from bacteria clinging to tubes near my heart. And my lungs were filled with fluid. I was drowning. I needed water pills to pee it out. More fluids would kill me.

The team never came back in. I was transferred to the ward and given Lasix. Over the next three days, the gurgles as I gasped each breath became less prominent. Eventually, I could speak more than a word or two between breaths. Then I was discharged with oral antibiotics.

C2 Tap

Once the antibiotics were complete, they scheduled me again. Time to assess my CSF levels and look for irregularity of flow. I've never stayed more still in my life. The needle dangerously close to my brain stem.

The needle went in just fine. Congenial chatting with the needle-bearer. An attempt to draw out fluid. A puzzled look. A call to the radiologist over speakerphone.

"It's dry." He looked at me and said, "I've never seen someone who literally had nothing to pull out."

"Makes sense," I said. "It feels like my brain is grating against my skull."

"It is."

Contrast went in just fine. Took its normal course around the brain and into the spinal column. There was nothing wrong with my brain's ability to circulate it. CSF just wasn't there to circulate. It was all spilling into my abdomen through my lumboperitoneal shunt, the tube in my spinal cord that diverted spinal fluid into my abdomen so my spinal cysts wouldn't stretch and paralyze me.

Needle out. Procedure over. Results—'normal'.

There was nothing for neurosurgery to do, except a valve on my shunt. And if they did it, they would own me too.

"You'll have to stay here for follow-up." A call to my neurosurgeon on his cell again.

"Come home, Kat. I'll do the valve. You don't need to be there."

"Yes, sir."

I wholeheartedly object to the concept of a person owning me. However, if anyone possibly could, it would be the man who had tried to fix me and saved my life, over and over the past two miserable years. My neurosurgeon was my own personal savior. He never stopped trying. I went home. And it was a very entertaining trip.

RPG (Random Plane Guy)

I had almost died at Mayo. I was working my way back home. I missed my flight, literally banging on the doors. They left. Rerouted.

One of the flights entailed me getting reseated on the plane. I don't remember exactly why the seat I was supposed to be in didn't work, but they put me next to this guy.

And so it went. And we were ridiculous from the first moment. Kind eyes. Clever jokes. Within seconds, I had delved into his mind and benign yet intrusive evaluation of pathology.

"Do you mind if I ask you a series of progressively personal questions?"
"Not at all. Please do."

The man doesn't need sleep. It's pathological while simultaneously hurting no one. Not caustic at all. Just honest and sincere. For no reason at all, we immediately confided in each other. We talked for hours. We talked about my cancer and surgeries and near death. We talked about incredibly nerdy references and videos. We talked about life and vulnerability. And we walked off the plane arm in arm.

My life seemed to be ever more a collage of the ridiculous. Whether they be horrific moments compiled or raucous humor in ridiculously ironic contexts, it kept going. The pendulum of pain and joy seemed ever present. And I savored the joy, still do.

We exchanged numbers. And we kept up. Our spouses think we are nuts and are utterly confused by the very strange friendship. As each shoe dropped, he was up and willing to talk. We found the positive in the most ridiculous places.

Zero judgement. Zero strings. Just sincerity. And inappropriate humor.

I called him at my next surgery. The valve placement I was preparing for on the plane home. Cam was deployed and the complicated one couldn't be troubled to walk down the hall. RPG dubbed him 'Vader'.

Further complications occurred and I trudged through each day. More scans, more investigation. When I found out about my benign brain tumor that might allow easy intervention, I called RPG. He was up. He didn't mind. We laughed about my 'good' brain tumor. I sent him a picture of my tumor. We laughed about how part of my imaging looked like a vomiting seahorse on MRI. He worked at a prominent spaceship organization. He worked the image into a PowerPoint the next day.

And so I just kept going. And he was always there. He was one of the very few in my life that wasn't exhausted or in denial of my ridiculous medical prison.

Fall 2012

My neurosurgeon had been deployed to Kandahar that summer. There was nowhere to turn. The headache wouldn't shake. We did an MRI and found the pituitary mass. Hope. We could intervene on that. Somebody could. Off to Johns Hopkins.

But they didn't, or wouldn't, intervene, and no one would tell me why. My peripheral vision lost. A suicide attempt. Atonement and voluntary admission to the psych ward. The Navy's wrath. That all bears a greater explanation.

The headaches wouldn't stop. I couldn't sleep. I was a shell of a human. The 'good' brain tumor we had found in August had defied my hopes and expectations. The Johns Hopkins consult was dragging on with no intervention and no reason why not. Months between visits and insurance approvals.

I went to dinner with a friend in November. I had just been broken up with by the complicated boyfriend. He had broken the news just as I got back from the ER after losing my peripheral vision. It was a well-known consequence of the very tumor we knew I had. They gave me high dose steroids, doubled my antidepressant, told me they couldn't operate on my pituitary mass (without why), and gave me TCAs for pain. TCAs are widely known in the medical community to be an easy and effective way to kill yourself.

I had no intention. After dinner I had the feeling that I should sleep on my friend's couch. But he had work. I'd be fine.

I went home. A glass of wine and a call with 'a friend'. I was low. My fight kept coming up empty, and no one would even tell me why they couldn't operate on my typically operable pituitary tumor to cure my vision deficit and pain. Steroids were the only thing that alleviated the pain enough to sleep.

My memory is thin. A discussion of pain. A consideration of the TCAs. A lapse of hope.

"If you cared more about your daughter and not screwing dudes…" It's the best I can do to recreate what she said to me. I remember protesting. Trying. I love Casey so much. I can't protect her. I can't take care of her. All I can do is sit on a couch or be functional for an hour here or there. I'm just trying to survive. I'm just trying to have something in life. It's all gone.

During the conversation, I took one of the TCAs. The pain was horrible. I took another. Low dose. Next thing I remember, all I can remember until I woke up in the ICU, was seeing pills in my hand.

My brain was swollen. In the time since I last perceived reality, I had seized and nearly died. A tube through my nose went down my throat. They had filled my stomach with charcoal to absorb the poison and save my life. My old chief resident was my attending.

I saw him, greeted him, and told him that I would voluntarily admit myself to the psych ward. I knew how this works.

Seriously! How did things get even worse?

Cam

Other than having Casey, no event in my life has ever meant so much. I was wheeled up to the psych ward as per protocol. I walked, as a physician, in the hospital I trained in, through a door that locked on the wrong side. I went to the desk for intake.

"Kat?"

"Yes."

"There's a phone call for you. They've been waiting."

"What?"

"In the common room. There's a call. He's been waiting."

"Hello?"

I don't remember what he said beforehand, how he told me it was him. I just remember Cam's voice: "I don't want to live in a world without Kat."

Everyone in my life was broken by my selfishness. I had disappointed them over and over again by not getting better. They were all suffering because I was languishing under the constant threat of death and debility. I was useless, incapable of mothering, no longer a functional doctor, and this man told me all he wanted was me.

We had played the game of play. We had made it all seem insignificant and without consequence. He had comforted me in the worst times of my life, and I didn't even know that he was my foundation. I wouldn't know for a while yet.

But I was loved. Totally without anger or aggression at what I had almost done, I was loved.

It would be roughly six months before I realized that he was the love of my life. But that moment changed my world.

Back to San Diego

After Christmas and New Year's on the psych ward, friends visiting me with disappointment, me avoiding my daughter so she didn't have to remember visiting her mom in these circumstances, they shipped me back. No more Johns Hopkins. No word as to why we weren't operating. They wouldn't let me log in and see my own MRI.

Nothing. Just "get your ass back here."

So I went. Farther from Casey again. At the mercy of the Navy. Now I had to check in with SARP (the Navy's punishment/treatment program). I had abused medications and almost died. I was a military leper to be kept track of. The news lamented how many military members killed themselves every day. And the Navy made sure that all of us that thought about it or tried it were taught a lesson for making them look bad. I don't know that the cycle necessarily applied to me. But the cycle was pretty damn clear.

Check in. Penance.

I don't really know why I wanted to stay in at that point. I didn't really want to. They were keeping me from my daughter. But it was what I knew. I felt terrible about how useless I was. They emphasized it further. I wasn't being separated anymore. I was being kicked out.

The Navy had prescribed me THC because I couldn't eat otherwise. It was all recorded in my notes. But smoking it meant I had betrayed them and was an addict.

Pot

I had been starving for years. I desperately wanted food. I would eat. And it would come up. Nothing would stay down. A gastric emptying study, radioactive eggs and imaging. My stomach wasn't working. Nothing I did worked. It was worse than when I was pregnant. Nothing would stay down. I was shrinking.

In 2012, February-ish, before the August brain tumor diagnosis and November suicide attempt, I had shrunken to a size two. I was naturally a size six, size eight at times. I bought new size two jeans. Nothing else would stay on. I stood up to go to the bathroom one day at my boyfriend's house. My new pants literally fell off me. There wasn't much of me left.

We tried Marinol. I could eat a little. I didn't have to survive on citrus and salt to keep the nausea at bay when I sat with friends at restaurants. I could take a few bites. The constant gnawing of hunger was slightly less agonizing. And medical marijuana was legal.

I got a script.

I'm not going to say that watching particular movies wasn't fun. But, generally speaking, I hated being dumb. My brain and mouth wouldn't connect on pot. I was locked in my head when I used it. But I could eat.

And all the sudden, my pants didn't fall off. I couldn't eat much, but I could eat something. I might just live.

The Toll

But when it didn't stop the pain and all the rest still happened, there was medical marijuana in my medication bag when EMS took me to the hospital for the suicide attempt. Thirty-four medications. All prescribed, including the pot. Opiates from years before I had never used. NCIS verified every script. And I was screwed.

Now, mind you, I screwed me. Pot saved my life. It made me stupid and I hated it much of the time, but it saved my life. 100% accountability here. But I'm only here to be accountable because I managed to stop starving.

Nonetheless, what I had to do to survive, with a legal prescription, meant I was enemy number one. I may have been defensive at first, but I'll absolutely take it now. I lived. My daughter has a mother. And even though it is legal in California, I have no interest in smoking it. Thankfully, I can eat a meal a day with prescribed meds and I don't need pot anymore.

I don't know if all this sounds resentful. I don't mean for it to. I appreciate the Navy's perspective. I just appreciate living and medical data more. Regardless, I was being out-processed from the Navy, General Honorable due to the context. They would have crucified me if they could have. They made it clear how despicable I was. But I was eventually able to move on with life, largely thanks to Cam.

Status Migraine

So, as it turned out, part of the reason for my excruciating pain, exacerbated gastroparesis (paralysis of stomach), inability to read due to eye dysfunction (ophthalmoplegia), and desperate nausea, was a 14-month migraine.

When I got back to San Diego, I went to see neurosurgery. Since my neurosurgeon was running Kandahar at the time, I met with another one. I asked him why they wouldn't operate on my adenoma (benign pituitary tumor).

"Has nobody shown you?"
"No. I keep asking, but no one will let me see it."

A look of puzzlement and a turning of the computer screen. "Look. It's naturally receding and we will have to shred your whole pituitary if we operate."

"Well, can we open the tentorium to alleviate the pain? Isn't there anything we can do."
"It's not abutting the tentorium."
"Then why am I in so much pain?"

"I mean, it could be a migraine."

"A migraine? What if it is? What can we do?"

"We could try DHE."

And we did. Dihydroergotamine. Three-day infusion. Nothing changed the first day. The second day I felt like lights were blinding, sound was deafening, and my nausea was even worse. The pain was blunted enough to acknowledge as head pain rather than a dagger in my skull. Day three: relief.

I had a 14-month migraine that drove me to try to kill myself. And we broke it.

Back to Work

Three weeks later, March 2013, I was back in clinic. It was a slow progression as meds and Botox kept my migraines at bay, but I was alive again. I could see. I could read. I could even eat a little. Sleep wasn't great, but I got some. Life.

And as I discovered that I wasn't wasting away in my own skin anymore, I started to realize how long Cam had been sitting by my side through the pain, at least when he could. There were a number of deployments in there. As I learned to live again, we were forced to face what we were doing.

I had every intention of moving back to DC to be with Casey as soon as I could. But as the months wore on and the out-processing stalled, we got closer and closer to my ex-husband getting new orders. Even if I moved to DC, he was going to try to take Casey elsewhere. The deal where he would move back to San Diego for split custody was looking less and less likely all the time.

But Cam knew Casey came first, and I knew Casey came first, so we tried to call it off, move on, and let life take its course. In short, we were being stupid. Because I wasn't even going to end up with Casey within the current plan, and who knew when the Navy would even let me out? Slow and painful is the name of the game.

Enter Sara.

Fourth of July

So, after not dying, and getting back to San Diego in 2013, I made a new group of friends. Many have come and gone, but a couple of them have weathered the last ten years with me and Cam. Those friendships were forged in 2013. And one of those friends called utter bullshit on me and Cam on the Fourth of July.

"You guys are stupid. You love each other. Why waste it?"

"She needs to go to Casey," said Cam.

"I have to leave," I said. "It can't work."

Safe to say that, not only did Sara not buy it, but she made sure that Cam and I acknowledged our own stupidity.

We told each other that night that we were in love with each other. We've never turned back.

Not long after, my ex-husband got orders to Portugal and I knew I had to let Casey go with him for the experience. After surviving physical hell, I had emotional hell to face.

There is zero chance I would have gotten through it without Cam.

We were engaged a year later and married shortly thereafter. He and Casey adored each other then and have since. And after Portugal, Casey came home.

My Daughter

There has been no greater joy in my life. And there has been no greater despair than acknowledging when I could not be for her what I lived to be. In the daily moments of three years, I had to let her be with my family to know that I would not inadvertently cause her self-injury by my neglect. That sort of realization is more crushing than I can possibly relay. I was there for her every moment I could be. And my parents were there for every moment I couldn't.

I visited her at my parents' every weekend that the Navy would allow me. I lay prostrate in bed, her playing on me or next to me, every moment I could. The self-loathing was beyond words. I sent her toys. We talked on the phone or Skype any moment possible. I would crumble in tears after each hang up.

Even once I started to rebuild my life, once I convinced the state licensing that I was well again in 2014, every one of my patients knew that I would leave the room for however long if my daughter called. I had a singular duty. Though medicine and giving all too much to my patients has been my seemingly entire self, there was a greater element. My daughter came first. Not a single one of my patients ever objected.

. And eventually, I was rebuilt, largely though Cam. When Casey moved to Portugal in 2015 with her dad—initially anticipated for three years and then actually for two—it crushed me. There was no way I could say no to her having that life experience. It was 100% wrong for me, and the right thing for her, or so I thought. I let her go and fell into a deep depression, all the while giving myself to my patients. All the while learning to trust again by letting Cam know my despair.

And yet when she did call, when I managed to get her on Skype, the couple of weeks at Christmas or months in the summer, we talked. We addressed the pain and the suffering. We talked about getting through. I learned to breathe shallowly all those times I was dropped off at the airport, my daughter sobbing, "Mama, don't go." And I went. I hated myself. I sobbed and I curled up. But I did it again the next time, just to have moments before those crushing departures.

And we grew. We became. And one day, she even came home. I had missed five years for the most part, apart from calls and vacations and weekends and despondent and broken self. Apart from the love of my life that I could only nurture for moments at a time for a while, trusting that she was being taken care of.

And yet, six years after finally getting her back, we sit here facing my cancer again, and with smiles on our faces. We've learned how to grieve and fight. And now I have the hope for a cure, and at the very least a really good plan. We aren't crying. We are smiling. We've made it this far and we keep on fighting though each day, loving each day that we get, because we can.

We know the fear, but we've always known the fear. Since I left my then husband in 2011, since I was dying from the time she was one to three, we pushed through and made it work. We found each other every moment we could. We found Cam. And he found us. And gratitude pervades our lives in a way that I simultaneously wish on everyone and would never curse anyone to have to earn.

Rebuilding

During the time she was gone, I got out of the Navy, rebuilt my career, and discovered through great pain how to live again. It involved counting down six months of Cam's deployment while I worked at an internal medicine clinic targeted by the Sacklers. It involved trying, failing, and succeeding at being a stepmom. It involved the terror of facing actual life again.

You would be surprised how difficult it is to decide to live again after years of merely trying to survive. Once all has been lost, the fear of hope is more paralyzing than actual paralysis. There was absolutely no way that I could stand losing it all again. That meant that building it all back up felt like dragging the weight of my own pain and stacking it into a precarious cliff. Many days I stayed in bed. Many days I heaved and retched. Hope was the last thing I had to lose and I was playing Russian roulette.

Part of building meant flexing my medical muscles again. I did. I was helping people.

Helping people in Hemet, which was effectively a third-world country 90 minutes from San Diego. It was poor. Destitute even. Big Pharma-employed reps brought lunch every day and extolled the virtue of long-acting opiates for back pain. Patients came in regularly seeking them. Not from me.

I made many of those reps cry. Breaking down the mechanism, discussing how inappropriate opioids are for chronic pain, what it does to your pain tolerance, how it worsens the pain. How they were liars. I was told to back off. After all, they were bringing us lunch. So I brought my own lunch and stayed away. I couldn't listen to it.

But it was a building me back again job. I just had to weather it. I just needed my loves back. And, in time, I extricated myself, got back to my loves, and built a career going to the people that can't make it to appointments. Rare opiates outside of hospice. No selling one's soul. Just getting my life back and bringing care to people who needed it...saving Medicare hundreds of thousands of dollars a month in the process.

Back to life. Back to living. Back to gratitude. Back to serving. For nearly a decade...until my legs didn't work again.

COVID

Before I get to now, I need to touch on the time between 2017 and now. My last follow-up with my neurosurgeon was in 2017. My full neuroaxis MRI was stable.

As I walked in for my follow-up, back into that office that so often acted as the harbinger of doom, I was met with kind eyes.

"I still can't believe that you are alive. If anyone tries to put a scalpel to your back again, they'll have to go through me."

I smiled and nodded. I filled him in on my new life, a doctor in nursing homes. He smiled with pride and asked about Casey.

"We got her back."
"Who's we?"
"My new husband and I. He's wonderful. He stood by me through it all."

My neurosurgeon's face was full and beaming. He was proud of me. And he knew I was only there to succeed because he had worked his ass off to keep me alive.

We decided on annual surveillance, maybe even pushing it out to two years if it stayed that way. I didn't get another MRI for 5 years. Life got complicated. I couldn't face my past for a while. I just needed it to stay in the past.

I considered getting an MRI in 2020, but then COVID hit. I had made a lot of progress starting to reconcile my life and be present in the present right up until February of 2020.

We all share this trauma, so I will keep it brief. What happened in the coming months and years brought back the fear of death that I knew so well. But, fortunately, my own misfortune served to prime me for the path ahead.

I am a doc in nursing homes. When February 2020 hit, I was met with horrors that I could only reckon with because death, and the threat thereof, was so familiar to me. When no one else would go in, I didn't step back. We saved countless lives and watched many others suffocate in front of us.

We had no tools. No data. Everything was new. We did our best and it turned out that was a lot better than many. My own illness cued me in to some of the things I saw.

I remember when we lost an 102 year old. There were outbreaks everywhere and she had not only survived the

Spanish flu as a child, but she survived COVID. And then she stopped eating. We told ourselves and each other that she simply had enough and wanted to go.

But then there were others. They didn't choose not to eat. They simply couldn't. As we all know, there was little data and no tools at the time. I knew the misery of not being able to eat, and so I figured I would try Reglan. I've been on it since 2011 and it's the only reason I can eat a meal a day. It was worth a shot.

I haven't lost a single patient to starving to death since April/May of 2020. Post COVID gastroparesis. I still treat it all the time. And I wouldn't have even thought of the treatment if it hadn't been for my own path. I've shouted from the rooftops to get people to listen, but studies still haven't even acknowledged it. At 1 tablet before bed in many dozens of patients, I've still not seen a single case of tardive dyskinesia (the feared side effect of the medication and the reason for doctors' pause).

And that wasn't the only thing. I had an asymptomatic case of COVID in February of 2020 and my daughter and I isolated at the time, particularly given her low grade fever and one stark red eye. Data out of Wuhan weeks later reflected that this was acute infection. But, all the sudden, two weeks later, my heart was beating out of my chest. I bought a smart watch. My heart rate got up to 210 while I was sleeping. It only ever happened when I was relaxing or resting. My heart rate while working or exercising was normal. I started to see it around me.

A paradoxical sinus tachycardia. Effectively, fast heart rate when relaxing, when it was supposed to be low. Probably the vagus nerve. Triggered by the parasympathetic state. It was supposed to be the opposite of 'fight or flight', but my heart didn't seem to know that.

And it has proven to be real. I saw it, treated it with beta blockers. Advocated for my own. Weaned most patients over a year or so and myself over three. Just last fall, it became clear in the data. And my symptoms got better with every shot and booster.

Regardless, my path had a purpose. I wasn't afraid to run into the fire. And I wasn't afraid to look for odd syndromes or treatments. It has served me and my patients well. And I'll leave it there.

The trials of 2020 and beyond meant I didn't seek surveillance MRIs. I was too busy trying to fight the fight. And I had to work hard to keep the images of that fight, the last breaths and the withering bodies, the desperation and the fear, from behind my eyes. I didn't have it in me to examine the possibility that my initial reason for fear lurked within. I avoided follow-up.

Again

Late 2022 hit. My legs had started failing again. I hadn't sought surveillance for years because I simply didn't have the strength to look. And reality came to bear. A close friend got terrible news that overlapped with my own history. If I didn't look, then I could be submitting to the trajectory that I've been combating with every ounce of my soul for damn near 20 years. It was time.

It took me forever to get the MRI. My PCM wasn't listening and too many people (who don't understand the nature of malignant ependymomas) figured I was 'fine' because I wasn't dead. I've always known that it would come back for me, and my legs failing was the punch in the gut to remind me of what I've tried to put out of my mind. And my friend's fight reminded me that it is all too real.

I got the MRI. It was read as 'negative' for recurrence. Reassuring. That is, until I looked at the images myself. 'Negative' is not the word I would use. My mind began to spin.

You know, every case, every patient, you tell yourself that your mind is holding true, that your judgement is correct. You tell yourself that all of the objective facts that you are putting together, combined with your intuition, make the case. They guide your judgement. They provide your confidence.

And then it's you. It's your family's future. It's everything you have ever known or want to be. And all of those moments where you told yourself you didn't really know, that you weren't so sure, that the facts weren't as clear as you were seeing them...they come back. Mental chaos and second guessing.

I needed help. I needed to not be my own doctor. I sought out City of Hope for an appointment. I wasn't the only one who considered 'negative' a misnomer. And I happened upon someone that not only appreciated where I was coming from, but gave me a place to go.

City of Hope

It was the middle of the night and I was fighting going to sleep. I was racked by my fear and inability to get anyone to listen. I was spinning and digging into my own brain for a way out. A commercial came on for St Jude or something of the sort. I remembered that I referred the most challenging patients in Hemet, who had no place to go, to City of Hope. I looked them up and added the search term 'ependymoma'. Multiple specialists. I called.

I referred myself. I explained my situation. I didn't actually think I would succeed. And they were receptive. They had appointments. They even had an appointment when we would be nearby at a cabin. My husband and daughter were going to ski and play in the snow. I had given up skiing. My legs couldn't do it anymore. I booked the appointment. They could play and I would go get help.

I revised the synopsis of my history. It was too complex to go in blind. If anyone was going to help me, they would need to know that no one can operate. They would need my MRIs. They would need to know that I already didn't fit into paradigms. I should've been dead long ago. And yet I want to live.

Skull Hole

I sat waiting in the room. I didn't even bring my cane. I was walking okay that day. A woman my age walked in.

"Thank you for the summary. I've read it five times and I still have questions."

I chuckled. "Absolutely. I'm a shitshow. But I'm the luckiest unlucky person you'll ever meet."

She smiled. She introduced herself. Asked clarifying questions about my history. Told me she had never seen anyone 17 years out from a WHO Grade III Ependymoma. She was impressed that I was alive. I felt at ease simply being appreciated for that.

"I want to stay alive and upright and I don't think my MRI is negative."
"I agree."

I smiled appreciatively. "…but I think radiation will paralyze me and turn my communicating arachnoid cysts into non-communicating ones."

"Yes, me too."

"Chemo isn't an option."

"Right."

"So what do we do?"

"That's why you're here."

"Yes."

"For the CAR-T study."

"What?"

"I'll just drill a hole in your skull and—"

"Hold on. You can drill a hole in my skull if you want, but I don't know what you are talking about."

A look of shock. "That's why you're here to see me."

I was confused. "The appointment time worked. I don't know what you are talking about."

"No, I mean, that's how you got to ME."

"Um, the appointment time worked. I still don't know what you are talking about."

She looked like she was about to have a stroke. We went back and forth. I had absolutely no idea who she was. It was pure serendipity.

"I'm the lead researcher on an ependymoma vaccine clinical trial. That's why you're here. That's why you wanted to see me."

I just laughed. Her shock turned into confusion turned into stupor. And then she laughed too.

"See. This is what I mean. This is the sort of shit that happens to me. This is why I'm alive."

So we talked. "The data looks like they can eradicate ependymoma with a vaccine. They take a tissue sample, take your blood, spin out your T cells, program them to target a protein specific to your cancer, and then give it back to you as a vaccine through a skull hole port (Rickman valve) to cure you."

For 18 years, I've wanted a chance at not death, never knowing how far death was, never knowing how long I'd be upright, never knowing if I could even imagine a long term future. But this appointment time sure as hell worked out.

We laid out a plan. Spinal tap, maybe PET scan, but a definite need to look. And I needed to hunt down my old pathology slides. Unbelievable hope. And yet the simultaneous recognition that a renowned neuro-oncologist who specializes in my cancer thinks it's back.

Relief

I got back to the cabin, thrilled. I told my daughter all about the cancer vaccine that I'll get if I need it. I think both of us understood that the cane I was using to walk into the room made that suggestion. My husband looked more confused, as if to say "are you telling me you have cancer?"

I clarified myself, "We don't know I have cancer, we just know that I might and we need to look, but that we have a cure available. This is incredible."

For people who haven't lived 20 years in my skin, that's not terribly reassuring. To me it was the greatest gift I could ever be given. The hope of living a full life. I called my best friends and family.

And so, with this tool available, I had the courage to look. I met with UCSD Neurology, who immediately said that I needed to get to neuro-oncology. My crappy insurance declined the referral. Cam and I talked about it, and decided to buy my life. I got better insurance, scheduled with neuro-oncology, and scheduled the Interventional Radiology guided lumbar puncture. I now had two neuro-oncologists who agreed my cancer was back.

The freedom of knowing the vaccine is out there quickly dissolved into the reality of what I was likely facing. My hope was renewed and my dedication to look strengthened, but the weight of it all hit like a brick wall. It was time to tap and acknowledge the reality of my fears. In order to face it again, I had to reconcile the past. So I started writing my story. I put my pain and fear on the page. I tried to leave it there. And now, having done that, I need to face the present.

I have the luxury of looking back at having survived. The security that the retrospectoscope brings. But now that I'm going to face it again, I have to face the suffering of not knowing if I'm going to make it. I've done it before, and I'll try to do it again. And Cam and Casey would have to weather it with me.

Guilt and Fear

I am terrified to make them suffer this with me even more than I am terrified of what is to come. I have to acknowledge not just the hope, but the reality of the fear, with them. Even though I have been striving and fighting for the moment where I can get this information, I don't know that I am prepared to tell them what might be ahead. Looking for cancer is scary as hell. I have tried to prepare them, but I'm not sure they are ready for what it means to look.

I have been working toward this moment, trying to reconcile the past. I have walked myself through the most trying times of my life. I even managed to get to the place where Cam saved me from me. I haven't quite captured that the most important part of Cam helping me rebuild myself has been the ability to be my daughter's mother.

Not just a mom. Not just the act of it. But being the person who waded through the filth and the pain with her. The mother that found the person I wanted to be for her. The moments where I let her know how flawed I am, and people are, for the sake of her future self-forgiveness. For the sake of being, whether or not I am here with her, or them.

And along the way, the two people that compose me found each other. We all found ourselves and each other within an ungodly amount of pain, truth, humor, and love. And so, as we face every single day, none of us are afraid to face those things with each other. No matter who we are on what day, we are allowed, we are understood, and we are grateful. And we will do it together.

Allowing fear and pain while you live in the consequences of its frailty is a Herculean task. But somehow they do that for me every day. I do it for them, too, but it never feels like a chore. They are everything outside me that I cannot be. They are so much more than I am. I'm just helping to paddle the boat. A boat that should have sunk decades ago. But I can't shake the guilt of making them suffer with me again.

Though Casey and Cam have had their perils, which I take as my own while trying to remember that I cannot, part of me wanted to spare them from the now again. But it is literally impossible. I cannot be here for them and not allow them me. So I shut down the ghosts and the demons that tell me how much I hurt them by being human, and I share. Somehow we feel empowered by it and the irrational mind cannot make it an unfair burden.

They just want to be informed. But, here we are again, I am in charge of the informing, the framing, the breaking down. And in this moment I'm not sure I can. I can't even face my own fear in this moment. How can I reassure them when I am terrified myself?

The Breakdown

February 2023, the night before the tap, writing to myself:

Tomorrow they will sample my cerebrospinal fluid. It's agonizing. Putting a needle through my dura, even with Interventional Radiology guidance, pushes on the effective tamale shell around my spinal cord and nerves. Those nerves are encased in scar tissue. The moment you push on the shell, the tissue pulls on my tethered spinal nerves. There is an electric pulling and stress that threatens their very integrity and my ability to walk, remain continent, or maintain organ function. It's not a pain that can be described. And yet, not only does it exist, but I will experience it again in a number of hours. That being said, I've survived 80+ times before over the years, just not in a decade.

Beyond the momentary pain, which I can withstand, the question of damage remains. Every time they do it, it feels like someone is skewering the nerve distribution like a hot poker. And I can only hope that function outlasts the pain.

But let's get past the process and focus on the outcome. There are two: the fluid they remove will either contain the cells of a spreading cancer or will not. If it doesn't, then cancer likely remains but remains hidden. This is, of course, the preference. Ependymomas can be insidious for quite some time, and may not form a mass for a while. Ironically, I need that mass.

But if there are no positive cells for now, no radiation, no cancer vaccine. More time to think and wait. Positive cytology and it's a whole other game. Radiation. Hope for the vax if we can secure a tissue sample that allows staining. My 2005 slides are long since gone. They only keep them for ten years. I'll keep trying, but hope isn't high. The lab just disregards my requests. Without a tissue sample there's no cancer vaccine. All the tools at my disposal, and no ability to use any but the rudimentary pro-mutation radiation rays.

We could try just to irradiate my lumbar spinal nerves, but, as I've said, ependymomas are insidious. If it's in the fluid, it's in my whole neuroaxis. And remember that I have a lumboperitoneal shunt. Those cells have been delivered to the surface of my visceral organs for at least a decade.

So tomorrow we just do what has to be done. My brain will have to wait for more data. I just have to sit. I know I can do it, because I have. But the prospect feels figuratively paralyzing while the process is potentially literally so. None of that changes what is, what has to be done, or the reality of waiting. Again.

All the Hells Before

Post-tap: What I learned today is that the misery of the past isn't always mimicked in what seems to be the unavoidable present. It was the least painful lumbar puncture I've ever had. And I cried on the table, having an anxiety attack beforehand. It was quiet sobbing and sniffling, mild shaking that I couldn't control. But it wasn't the stoic and resigned person I try to be.

I don't know if the nurses or the doc heard me. They didn't seem to mind. No attention was drawn to it.

I haven't been skewered in a decade. And I wasn't really skewered today. He found a good pocket, got his 18ccs, and I was on my way. I apologized a couple times instinctively for the inevitable wail. And they weren't threatened by it. I withstood what I needed to. They did their needed work, and they got me my CSF so that we can figure it all out.

I shook a bit. Each leg contracted excruciatingly when triggered, but I was reminded to breathe, my delicate sobs were weathered, and the job got done. My brain only felt a little low afterward. Nothing like when it was dry. I barely even felt like my eyes were being pulled on in my skull. 18 cc wasn't bad.

And my blood smear came back from pathology. No evidence of cancer cells. As I was looking, I discovered my white and red blood cells in my CSF were effectively normal and my glucose and protein were nothing of concern. It'll be a few days before we know about cells in my CSF. But it felt manageable again. The fear and chaos were gone.

I've told myself repeatedly that I refuse to die a thousand deaths. But when you anticipate a procedure that has left you screaming for hours on the table. When you remember all the times, likely 80 or so, that people poked into your spinal column, drawing out CSF from 5 or six sites, time and time again, the agony withstood becomes the expected.

It must have been twice in 2006, once or twice 2007, 2008 I think once, two or three times in 2010 before the world fell down. Cyst after labyrinthine cyst. Spot after spot. Hours each time. No real choice but to suffer the pain to get the information. Hours trying not to scream. Many moments screaming, none of it voluntary.

But the status quo isn't where we are. I was reminded of that today. There are plenty of 'agains'. But they are not equivalent. They are not unsustainable. Hell, if we have to do this every year, I can do it.

And that's where the decision tree settles right now. I'll do radiation if I must. I'll start the clock on the likely 10–15 years before secondary cancer if I must. But if it is still hiding, what am I willing to withstand to get the best shot at finding it every so often? This. I can withstand this. I can withstand today.

Preliminary Results

It took weeks, not days. Weeks of desperately trying to distract myself. Weeks of hoping to God that the pit of despair wasn't near on my path. Trying not to imagine a world where my daughter is without me again. The agony of time passing.

One cell. One abnormal cell, that is. Second pathology review pending. But, in my position, we are fundamentally at a 'one or zero' state. With the likelihood of recurrence of a WHO Grade III Ependymoma, one cell is enough. No longer in remission.

And yet I'm not surprised. The livedo reticularis (vascular pattern rash) on my calf for a couple months now was a wave from the cancer. "Hi, I'm here."

So, we found one cell in there. One identified cell, severely abnormal, floating in the cerebrospinal fluid surrounding my brain, spinal cord, and spinal nerves, is sufficient to know the inevitable is here. The choices kept cycling in my mind.

I could irradiate. Any existing cells would just be inaccessible longer and the communicating scar tissue cysts encasing the nerves would likely become non-communicating, accumulate pressure, and stretch the nerves in the walls to the point of failure. Paralysis. Or…we could do high volume taps every few months, try to capture the cells. It was endurable this time. I can do it again. I can suffer the pain of looking for the benefit of not being paralyzed yet. More time walking the dog with my husband, going to Paris, standing upright for a hug with my daughter. I can do this.

So, we'll see. I can't really be despondent. I knew it was there. This is just another wave from the cancer. I'm grateful for the detection that didn't falsely reassure me. I'm glad a year won't pass before we look again. "I'm grateful. I'm grateful. I'm still here."

Pathology

It wasn't just abnormal. It looks pretty mean. And it was ovoid, was it replicating?

The meeting with my neuro-oncologist went well. She understood why I don't want to irradiate. She said, "Only one cell."

My response was, of course, "I'm pretty sure we didn't happen to capture the only one. There are others."

So we talked about how to look, the lack of urgency, but the confidence that it's very likely back. She threw out there a surveillance schedule, thinking she was being too aggressive for me. "I'll look as much as you want. We can tap every few months to give my nerves time to recover. I'm just glad that we know to look."

There isn't much we can do with one cell. Typically you do two stains at minimum. Any effort at staining it for the marker of malignant ependymoma isn't there with one. All I can do is learn to sit with it and try to get more cells when we can.

I've talked and thought a lot in my life about the concept of sitting with the devil. Well, I'm effectively doing that with the biological devil of death and brain cancer, with a side of paralysis, at the moment.

I've been many things. I've made plenty of mistakes. I have tried to own them and to accept those of others while still drawing lines as to what I can take. Ironically, that never works with myself. And I sit here grappling with how to live with my cancer. I know I can't beat it. I can try to corral it. I can try to move mountains to work myself toward the cure...the cure that I can only get if I can get destroyed slides from 2005 or from a new mass, if I give it time to accumulate.

Around and around in my head. If I can get enough tissue, I can get into a study that can save my life before my legs fail and I don't meet criteria for the study anymore. If I can provide enough evidence that the thing everyone knows is coming back for me is back, then I can get the cure. But, if we get tissue it's because the monster is trying to eat me again. Fleeting thoughts of hoping that there's something to biopsy. My irrational mind greedy for the supposed cure. But what I really want is not to need it. I want to stay in this purgatory: nothing definitive, nothing to fight, nothing to take over my life again, at least not yet.

"I Love You, Mama"

So we have concerning results. I've been here before. I need to sit with it, to allow time, and to avoid making conclusions when my trajectory is not yet known. In the meantime, I'm not only a desperate cancer patient. I'm a mom to a 13 year old. I'm the wife to the love of my life who won't make it long without me. They are trying not to show their fear.

And I'm trying not to picture them mourning me in my head.

I'm my daughter's protector. I consider myself too often the only defense, but my daughter is becoming. And she is fabulous. But she still needs me. I need to be here. And I would really like to outlive my cats. I still need to protect, even if I can't necessarily protect myself. So we all keep pushing on, dealing with each moment as we can.

Casey happily said, "I love you sooo much!"

Of course, I responded, "I love YOU SOOO much!"

And then she said, "I hope the study works," and walked away. I buried my head in my hands knowing I really didn't have any words to make it better.

It is utterly ridiculous to say it, and indisputably true. Meandering and suffering through the suspicion of cancer is the best pain you can hope for when you are like me. It was always going to come back. We think it's back. But it is nearly imperceptible it's so low grade. The hope is to keep it that way.

The more time we spend not knowing means we don't know. Once you know, it's a whole other game. My goal is to be vigilant enough that we simultaneously allow medicine to advance and act as soon as humanly possible once it declares itself. It's a great plan. And it entails agonizing patience.

And that patience bears out in my daughter's eyes and fears. I sit with it every minute. I try desperately to alleviate others' pain, as I always have, and sometimes it is beyond what I can help. Other times I can't even process my own need for help.

I'm here again. With cancer comes the fear of what you are doing to those around you.

It is completely unfair to phrase it that way. And it is totally honest to phrase it that way. The conundrum gets to the heart of what cancer means to people's lives.

Power is at the heart of it. You need it, you must find it when it is taken from you, you must let it go. It's impossible. And yet so much of life only makes sense in that context.

I will not ever say that I am grateful for cancer. It's evil, destructive, and sometimes it feels like it dissolves your soul. But it also frames things in a way that we all need. It makes you understand that you will never really be able to control things, that it's fruitless to seek that control, and that self-compassion is the most important tool any of us will ever have.

I am languishing in the time between taps. The time between data points. The not knowing trajectory. And I need to let myself. Not knowing is infinitely better than a definitive diagnosis so much of the time. But the road signs keep telling me that diagnosis will come, and I feel smothered by it.

The Sound

The slapping of feet. It somehow catches me off-guard every time. Cam doesn't look anymore. He knows the sound. Starts with the right. Left often follows. Worse uphill. Sometimes gets better on flat.

There's no ignoring it. My legs are straining. I harken back to the cadence of pushing my wheels. The rattling of the wheels when I pick up speed. I don't want to be in the chair again, but I want to stay here. And I should be grateful for the ability to, if I can get it, however I can get it.

Dragging leg, flopping feet. Inching forward. "I'm grateful. I'm grateful." Sometimes I'm more angry than grateful, but I can breathe through it, put my chin down, and slog forward. Still upright. "Stay upright. Do it as long as you can. You're still here."

I remember Casey when she was five. 2014. She still remembers. She hates wheelchairs. They aren't toys. They are mama's future legs. She pushed me in that chair up the hill.

We were at the Wild Animal Park. It's a massive hill. My legs failed at the bottom. I don't even know how I miraculously found an abandoned wheelchair. It was just there. And my legs wouldn't go. She was visiting me because I couldn't take care of her all the time but I was getting better. And my legs went limp as they do.

I told her there was no option. She said she didn't want to, that she couldn't. I said we would do it together. We just had to. I couldn't make it.

So I sat, removed the brakes, and told her to time her pushes with me. I would mind the brakes if we backslid. We just had to.

And we did. We got up the hill. It was terrible for her. Terrible for me. My poor daughter. She was so little. And I was broken. I wanted to be able to put her on my lap and do it myself. But I couldn't. And I don't remember how many hours it took. But it hurt.

In retrospect, we could have sat, brought attention to the problem, and someone would have driven us up the hill in a cart. But not at that moment. We were stuck. I was broken. We had to do it together. And we did. And, honestly, we have since. We still talk about that day.

So, back here in 2023, I get my miles in every day. I walk 5–10 miles each day. I take what I can get. I grunt through the feet slapping. The inching. The fighting. The trying not to know what's coming. I don't know. It's changed so many times. All I know is the fight. So we do it together.

Cam knows the look, knows the grip. Knows when to ask if I want him to go ahead and get the car, knowing I'll refuse. We push forward. It's all we can do. And I don't even want to know what it means not to be in this place. It's been damn near two decades.

But when I'm not in this place, I'm probably gone. As much as it hurts in the moment, I want more of this.

Pushing On

I don't know now and I didn't know then. They were so sure I would die. I tried to take each second as it was. I'm back there. It's been six months of fear again. I believe we don't know. I also fear we do. And the slapping of feet reminds me.

We'll look again soon. May. We'll tap and scan. I might ask for a PET. If we can find a mass and get a biopsy then I can try for a clinical trial. If I let it grow, I might win.

So every day I try to live my wonderful, cursed, lucky, amazing life with a daughter who I worship and who embodies everything good in life. I kiss my gorgeous husband who taught me to love again. I try to fend off the fear that I'm going to leave them. I try to fend off what may become of them in their grief.

And so we've been taking vacations. Making time. Taking time. Living together. We've been putting hope in the forefront and pretending that we don't all have our fears behind our eyelids every blink, every move.

I buckle. Not just emotionally. My right leg just goes sometimes. I can't bear weight. I try not to fall. I use whatever I have to hold fast. I take a moment and test it out, breathing deep. They see me. They wait. They take my cues.

I don't want help. I don't want to need it. I assess the risk, and I lock my knee, hoping the left will hold. Every time it happens is a time we just try to put that moment aside and hope the next is better.

Every day I test my legs at the side of the bed in the morning. There is no jumping out of bed. There hasn't been for twenty years. The bad days come and go. That is the best I can ask for. I have to learn to accept it again.

Not Gone

But I'm not gone. I'm not even going. It's still at the front of our minds. Assets? Taxes? Logistics?

Even Cam: "We can live in Belize on that." A chuckle and a smile.

"Love, we just got Casey back, we're not moving."
"But we could," and a smile and a duck around the corner.

I know he thinks about it. He's stronger than me, more practical. He can fight the thoughts off. But they're there. And I'm here. And I'm making it worse. I can't let my fear sleep. It's ever present.

The only time I don't think about it is when I'm working and helping others or laughing with Cam and Casey. And after I laugh I sit back and hope they can do it together, without me.

Confirmation Bias

But I have to remember that I haven't been fully diagnosed. It isn't everywhere yet. I haven't sampled the cure. I don't know a thing about outcomes yet.

And yet, since 27 years, I've been told I was going to die. And we all will. But, I've been conditioned that it will be premature. I've breathed through gurgling lungs, walked on failing legs, sampled death a time or two. I keep assuming my time is up, but I'm here.

I can't explain it. Maybe I've made autoantibodies to my own cancer. Maybe I'm just lucky. Maybe my actions have bought me credits with a higher power I don't give enough credit to. I just don't know. But I'm burning time in a current wonderful life convinced that my time is going to be up soon.

And while I live this blessed time and unbelievable joy, I'm overcome by fear of what is to come and pain not yet imposed on those I love.

The Load

There's a lot about it all that I have begged people to feel with me. But I don't think that's right. They're lucky. They don't know yet. That time when life gets real. Your age at that moment determines a lot of things. Most importantly, it determines the reactions of those around you.

There's some threshold in the 40s that people are able to cross.

"It's real now."
"We're getting older."
"Our parents are facing the end."

It allows you to let it in without it breaking in through the glass and the wall and the ceiling. It's different.

And when it happens later, it almost feels like an 'of course'. But the pain and struggle are still there, and it's almost an insult that there's an 'of course' involved. To many, it isn't 'almost'.

Now, I am more than happy to talk about the spectrum of each in any way that I can fathom. And, as a doctor to geriatric populations that has witnessed people in their 20s die of cancer, and other teens and twenties have their legs blown off or their cognition blown out, I can probably find a place that can approach true empathy.

But, dare I say, it was different when I faced death in my 20s. I had the unbelievable fortune to survive, and am forever grateful. But so few people understood. "You're young"; "It's going to be okay." Choose your platitude, genuinely felt, that reminded me that no one has context for me. It's was an unanticipated blow after surviving the avalanche.

But I lived with it. And I decided how many I would even attempt to let in.

Eventually, life set in again. Joy, hope. They became a thing again. Every feeling that I wasn't too numb to feel made me remember the life before. And then I had to decide to believe whether I could live again. When I tried to believe back in 2013, the fear of hope was crippling. It was the last thing I had to lose. I'm desperately afraid of knowing that place again.

Distraction

My May MRI was last weekend. I was worried and nervous. My daughter needed community service hours, so we planned to walk the beach the morning beforehand to get some time in together doing good. Beach air before the MRI sounded like a good idea.

But my cat had had a swollen chin and gums for a few days. I figured that he just got stung by a bee or bitten by a lizard. I woke up that morning to his snuggles and saw his gums. Necrosis. Not good. I called and made an appointment before we were off to clean up the beach. Probably an oral abscess or broken tooth.

So we walked the beach, cleaned up plastic, got a smoothie, and went home for a bit before I was off to the MRI. I slept in the tube, as usual, and calmed myself knowing we had eyes on whatever is happening in my back. Then off to the vet.

"In older cats, this can be cancer."

Hold on, buddy, I don't need that word today. "It's an abscess," I said. I didn't have room in my brain for anything else. Antibiotics and steroids and plans for an extraction this week. I told myself it would be fine. He's only five.

I tried to chase the words away, reassure myself with my clinical knowledge of humans. There's no way The Boy is going away. It'll all be fine. All of this simply can't be happening at once. I refuse to lose him.

Days passed. My MRI results came in. Stable. I looked at the images. Better to my eye. Less hyperintensity of the nerve roots. Relief. I hadn't even really had time to worry because I was worried about Guy in the back of my head.

Encouraging. I'll get my tap Friday, hopefully one or less cells. We're good. He'll get his tooth out and we won't have to worry about crushing loss at this moment. The words to myself, "I want to outlive my cats," came back to my head. I know he's just a cat. Even if it is cancer, he won't have to live without me. I can make sure we don't let him suffer.

Wednesday came. I dropped him off. I had to hold him for the sedation because no one wants to get near him. He's a tiger in a fat cat's body. They sedated him and I was off to work.

I was in clinic at a facility where I had shut down one of the first outbreaks in 2020.

Absolute hell then. Terror. Quiet anxiety attacks behind my mask. Watching people die.

And a different time now. More settled. Accepting of the horrors that come, albeit more slowly. Losing people to long COVID frequently, the new status quo. And the vet called while I was in clinic.

"We found a mass and biopsied it. Do you want us to send it?"

"Yes. Get path on it. Is he stable, can my husband pick him up?"

"Yes, he's ready when you are."

"OK. He'll be right there."

I kept seeing patients. Calm, balanced. It didn't set in. I wouldn't let it.

So, I got through the day and started driving home. The terror hit and the tears tried to. I just can't. I can't lose him. I can't take any more right now. Did I beckon this by wanting to outlive my cats? Am I just behind him? How am I supposed get through waiting for my Friday tap and results when my boy is going to be gone?

It may sound ridiculous. I don't equate my life with that of my cat. But there is only so much that a human can take. The death around me is constant. Friends ill and suffering. The fairly messed up aspects of daily life outside my household that I'm trying to contain. I just can't take losing Guy too.

He's my dude. He sits with me in the moments that help me get though all of this, bathing in the sun, shoving his nose into my hand at night to snuggle with me, galloping down the block to sit with me when he hears me listening to music in the yard. Is the world so freaking unjust that I have to face losing him and recurrence at the same time as all of the other suffering that just keeps seeping in?

I googled "Osteosarcoma in cats." If it was the jaw and necrotic that made the most sense. 3–5 months with amputation. One plus years with chemo. And then I stopped myself. I'm jumping. I don't know enough. Call the vet.

He called me back almost immediately.

"Did it look like it had invaded the jaw?"
"No, it looked granulomatous. Let's wait for the pathology."
"So probably benign? Could it have been an encysted foreign body with necrosis?"
"It could be. Let's just wait."

Soothed, for the moment. And also my brain screaming "FREAKING WAITING!"
But I'm ok. He's ok for the moment. Another friend diagnosed with breast cancer today. Commiserating words. We fought outbreaks together and now we can do this.

"We can beat it together. We MUST do Cancer Happy Hour."

Jokes and coping. Someone else in the fight. So many people in the damn fight. Another day.

Years

I try to remind myself that this isn't new. It isn't undoable. It just is. I've done it for a long time. Now isn't different. Just keep pushing through. The MRI was stable. The tap might be, too.

But it's a culmination of moments. A culmination of soul grating fear. What seems like a lifetime of trying to soothe those around me while I have absolutely no idea what is to come.

And the empathy for my friends. Caretakers. Patients. My husband and daughter. They take cues from us, the diagnosed, and we need to know how to ask for help and how not to ask for help if we can just contain it in our own minds for the time being. It's excruciating.

I tell myself that the best thing that I can hope for is limbo. That that's what I should crave and be satisfied with. There will never be another day of my life that I live without this fear. If I'm really lucky then I get to live years or decades with it. Not knowing forevermore is the best I can hope for.

I emailed my doc. "Can we make the pathology ASAP this time? It's grueling for me and my family to wait for weeks for results." But wait we will. This time won't be the last, even at its worst. All I can hope for is as many days waiting as possible, as many days between each crush as possible, as much time before the next change in symptom pattern to expedite the process.

I know I will never again have true relief. I haven't had it since October 30, 2005. All I really need is a lack of realization presented by the data. I must learn to live with it. Please, God, give me forever in this place of tolerable turmoil.

Friday Tap

It's funny. I'm not scared of the tap this time. It's tomorrow. It'll hurt. But I'm getting more oriented to doing this again. Back to the place where I understand that each step is neither the beginning nor the end. Just another day winding forward.

This time I don't have to wait weeks. The cytopathology is STAT this time. I'll know in days. Parts of me are more anxious. Others less. Back into the pace of one step at a time. Barring rampant proliferation, it won't really change much in terms of trajectory anyway. It's funny to desperately want to stay just as powerless as I am now. Just not more.

I went easy on myself this time. Cam and I are going to sit on a beach and await results. No demands, no obligations, just while away the time and try to take it. Casey isn't quite so lucky. She'll be with her dad trying to make the best of things and finish middle school work without us by her side. I wish I could change that part, but we've learned to live with the inevitability of not getting to control her environment, at least for now. She's almost 14, so her power looms, but she's accustomed to the powerlessness of waiting while contemplating what power means.

It's funny, not funny. She's incredibly mature. Our path has aged her beyond her years. But her whole life we've been in this battle together, trying to keep the joy of her age while allowing the maturity that comes when you had to be separate from 'your person' to live. It applies to both of us. She was two and I was 33. I couldn't take care of me so I couldn't take care of her. She had to figure out how to just keep being until she could get her mom back. Utter hell for both of us. And the most amazing union of spirits now that either of us could ask for.

But it's back. That thing that tried to take me. That thing that created death in my life and complications that I had to give everything to fighting. Even her. And she learned to wait. And she pushed through. And we got each other back. And now she has to wait without me to hear if she gets to keep me because it isn't 'my week'.

And she will. And it will hurt. And she will continue to grow. And soon we won't have to miss each other every other week anymore. We won't have to put off talking and hugging and coping together anymore. She'll just be here. And whatever we face, we'll do it together. It's the utter opposite of those awful years where she had to stay with her dad and all I could do was visit. The same Navy that kept me from going to her has now given her dad orders somewhere else so she's with me full-time. And I get to keep watching who she is becoming.

Graduation

I bought a dress recently. Pretty cheap but pretty. Worth a shot. It didn't fit so I left it on her bed. She wants to wear it to graduation. She finishes middle school in a few weeks. Off to high school just down the street. Walking to and fro on her own. Same house every day. Peace to be whatever teenage years bring her. Just the normal hard stuff.

So she tried it on. It fits well. I grabbed my college graduation dress from the closet for her to try, too. Fits almost as well. "Maybe I'll wear this to MY college graduation," she said. And each of us smiled outwardly while wincing inwardly. What will that time look like? Will I get to see it?

But neither of us can live like that. We oscillate. We worry. But, what we have is in front of us. The smiles and laughs and cerebral jokes. The goofiness. The days just being instead of wondering if there's a tomorrow.

Realistically, that's true for all of us. But it's been in our faces our whole lives together. We've never known life without it. And I can't remember my life before her.

Meaning started with her and built with Cam. The rest was just trying to get to them. So now, lucky as we are, we get to wait to hear how much of this we have left, and how much we're just going to have to cling to in our own minds.

But, as morose as that sounds, I'm not sad. Gratitude abounds once again. I don't know what we have in front of us, but I know we have this in this moment. And I know I will fight even harder than I ever have to keep everything that I ever wished for.

Ease with the Brutality of It

I alluded to my friend who was just diagnosed, to our plans to laugh it away over drinks while we fight. But it isn't just the diagnosed that have that challenge. It's those that truly understand suffering and momentary survival. It's not something I would ever wish on anyone, but it creates a part of you that enjoys life and peace so much more than you ever could before.

My best friend Ave, my sister. It's been 35 years now that we've been facing life together. And we are absolutely in it right now. It is far from pleasant. The recognition of fear, powerlessness, horror, willing obligation, just the ability to breathe. But it's Right. Every day. The dedication to fighting and growing in the midst of it. The trying to live while the world falls down. The recognizing the moments where it isn't collapsing and a cool breeze and sunshine just sustain you when you can get them. The rest of the time there's no real choice anyway. We do what we must.

It's what life actually is. What people run from constantly. And, somehow, some way, Ave and I ended up on proximal islands of that horror, breathing in the salt breeze and savoring it because we still can, no matter what the skies have in store for the other 99.9% of every day.

So we face what is. What each day is for each of us. Different and all too similar.

For her, it's less clear. Her life is second to second as she faces life's demands. As for me, tomorrow they'll stick another needle in. My legs will contract. I'll cry out in temporary agony. And after lying on my back for an hour so that the fluid doesn't get to leak out from around my brain again, I'll get up. And I may limp. I may hurt. But I will go on fighting the most worthwhile fight I could ever imagine with a man who is beautiful inside and out holding my hand, hugging my daughter, facing the music on the phone with my sister of 35 years, informing my family as they weather it with me, finding a place for the pleasure and the pain in the same existence, and going on...whatever that means. It's all we can do.

You Never Freaking Know

Wouldn't have bet on it. Took a vacation to Belize just so I could process bad news when it happened. Six months of terror for me and my family. My daughter figuring out how many of life's events I'll be there for. My husband thinking about how we'll spend our last months or years once the cancer rages. Me just trying to breathe. All of the other pain around us that reminds us we are lucky. How to process that, too.

That malignant cell from February. With my history and nonsensical survival, continued upright efforts, changes ongoing, it seemed a harbinger. Zero chance it was the only cell. I've said it before. And what these cells do is multiply. Even if we don't find them next time, we know they are there.

So we sat in Belize waiting. I was supposed to get the pathology back Tuesday at the latest. A telehealth appointment with my oncologist. And no results. Not yet. Those moments that my pathology results were delayed were hell. They must have found something. They must have found more cells. A secondary pathology review must be the source of the delay. I don't want to die.

I gave myself all the talks. My husband tried. And of those 86,000 seconds, I got away with a good 80,000 being fine. Maybe even 85,500. But the waves would come. The freaking weight of those moments that you let in...It's a lot.

And my husband, who fell in love with me when I was dying, who lovingly jabbed at falling for a single unemployed (I wasn't) mother in his wedding vows to the chuckles of all that attended, who is disgustingly practical about assumptions, he broke too. Here's the rub: he broke because of me, not the results. We didn't even have them yet. They ended up being good. But, in my head we had to be prepared, and the X and Y chromosomes clashed. And we were so angry at each other.

We're mad! We're being mad. We're angry. We're being angry. And sometimes we forget that all we really want is to not be afraid. And we don't know what to do with it.

Being angry at cancer doesn't seem to make much of a difference. But being angry at your spouse...well, that has real potential for satisfaction. So no. I wasn't happy being angry, he wasn't happy about being angry at me for being angry at him. Energy just got exhausted. And when I woke up in the morning I didn't even want to check. And when I got the good news that I couldn't imagine would actually occur, I didn't even want to wake him up to tell him.

"No malignant or atypical cells."

I just laid there. After a couple of minutes, I took a deep breath and reached over to him. He's deaf in one ear and was on the good one.

"Honey, no cells."

A shift and a waking deep breath. "What?"

"No cells, babe. No atypical or malignant cells. They didn't find more cancer." We both just sat there in silence for a minute, absorbing it.

When it comes down to it, the moments we get to be afraid together…all of us…are moments we would never trade for the alternative. I'll take as much of that as I can get. And I'll face each day with what I've got, dig in for more when the next wave comes, and savor the limbo with the people that sustain me.

I know it isn't gone. And I know it will probably win. But, for now I get a reprieve. Science will keep advancing in the interim. And when a mass does appear, we'll biopsy, drill a skull hole, and give the vaccine a shot.

But, for now, I'm going to live until I lose that option.

"No malignant or atypical cells," on this tap. Peace until November.

Appendix: Just in Case

As I have said, the day before my surgery in 2010, I knew things would get bad. I was pretty sure I would die. Casey was one year old. I sat down and wrote her bullet points to guide her though life without me. I found them a couple years ago and let her read them. She cried. And I told her, "I thought I was about to die when I wrote this to you. And now I've seen you grow and you embody everything I had hoped to teach you."

Over the years, I sat dying without her, I expounded on each point as I could, trying to leave as much of me as I could with her. I only got through the first four with the constant tumult of 2011–2012.

The entirety follows. The first four were my words to a toddler who would someday become a woman. And she is a young woman now. So instead of imparting my version of wisdom and perspective to her, Casey and I will expound on 5–26 together. She has her own wisdom and perspective now. Against all odds, we get to do this together.

1. However bad things get, laughing or crying will usually make you feel at least a little bit better (especially if you're laughing at an inappropriate comment).

When I was diagnosed with my cancer back in 2005, the neurosurgeons couldn't believe that I walked into the office to get my MRI results. The cancer should have paralyzed me long before it was detected. The surgery to remove it had an estimated 100% chance of lower extremity paralysis given that the tumor was wrapped around the nerves to my legs, not to mention those to my bowel and bladder.

Needless to say, I was terrified of what was going to happen to me and my legs. But, no matter what I did, the risks were going to stay the same. I had the president's neurosurgeon operating on me at Bethesda, and by the time I got home from the hospital, your dad's boss had gotten the letter faxed from my surgeon saying that he was going to need some time off to take care of me. Not only that, but they extended your dad in the Navy that day. He was originally supposed to get out a few months later, but my diagnosis turned our world around, so we needed to make sure we were financially secure, no matter what happened.

Our financial concerns were ameliorated, I had the best doctors working on me, and the rest was left to chance. Well, most of the rest. I could still control how I was going to spend the next six days, possibly my last on two feet. So I went dancing, and I joked with my friends about how 'tricked out' my wheelchair would be. Joe and Elaine and I drank wine and tried to come up with tasteless jokes that would keep us laughing instead of crying.

I did cry, of course, but not all that much. The tears didn't make me feel any better and didn't change what the outcome was going to be. I would have cried constantly, would still be crying, if it made any difference, but so would everyone else. The world would run on tears if that was true.

But, laughter is different. It actually makes you feel better. It starts a positive feedback loop that builds on itself. It reminds you that you still have some power. You can choose to laugh, and no matter how bad the joke, or how painful the truth behind the joke is, that laughter reminds you that things could be worse. They can always be worse.

2.   There's nothing like being kind to frustrate a jerk.

People who are being mean are usually doing so because someone was mean to them and they are projecting it outward. They may not even be conscious of how cruel they are acting, but feel wronged in some way, and being obnoxious to others is somehow supposed to make them feel better, feel bigger. They may not even know that it isn't 'normal' to put others down. But the reality is that being mean makes you smaller. It proves that you think so little of yourself that you have to step on someone else to feel significant, to feel like you matter. All that you prove is that you are insecure.

This is most dangerous in childhood and adolescence. Nothing quite makes sense, or made sense to me, at that age. The vulnerability of changing bodies, fluctuating neurotransmitters, and feeling alienated from your family and friends while simultaneously seeking approval from them is both exhausting and frustrating.

I was miserable and confused. When I was in middle school I wanted so much to belong to the cliques—which usually maintained leaders but traded followers on a weekly basis—that I even made fun of my best friend at one point to seek acceptance. I know 'best friend' is a term that gets used a lot, but I'm talking about Ave, who by now you know quite well.

At the risk of telling a story you've heard a million times by now, we were friends from the second we met. In fourth grade, I visited Maret, and it happened to be on the day of a field trip. I walked into the classroom of the lower school, was introduced, and immediately was either beckoned or walked over to Ave, and we have been best friends ever since. Family, really, with only a couple rifts in the twenty-some years since then.

Now, that is not to say that we did not make fun of each other, even from that very first day. It's is important to know the difference between a friendly joke that allows us to laugh at ourselves and each other, and a mean-spirited comment or action. When we were on the bus for the field trip the first day I met Ave, I fell asleep against the window in the back of the bus as I tried to fight off my carsickness.

'Fire! Fire!' Ave had crept up to me as I slept and startled me awake. I jumped up and looked around crazily. Everyone around me laughed. But most importantly, I laughed, and Avery laughed with me. It's still funny even now, actually. I wish I could have seen my face.

I went to Maret after fourth grade because I was being bullied at my prior Elementary school, and I was miserable. That, and DC public schools were pretty bad then, so my parents made a lot of sacrifices so I could have a good education. All in all, I was very happy to go to Maret, and made some incredible friends there. They are still most of my closest friends. But, I fell into the adolescent trap of throwing my true friend under the bus to gain acceptance by others at one point. Despite the fact that was when I was eleven, I still feel badly about it.

But what feels awesome is watching the wince in someone else's eyes when they make some rude comment to you and you shrug it off and move on, proving it inconsequential. It makes them feel even lower than when they started, and it shows that they are wasting their time when trying to mess with you. Even better, you can ask them if you offended them in some way, and put them on the defense while also being more constructive. It's a win, win.

If someone threatens you physically, however, it is another story. There is part of me that wants to say "Kick their ass, or call me to do it for you," but that is ridiculous. People that are willing to fight physically when it is not

175

unavoidable—or in the preservation of life or limb—can't be trusted not to fight dirty, and there is nothing casual or funny about trauma. Really bad things can happen easier than most people realize when violence is involved.

Luckily, I'm quite sure that your dad will make sure that you can fight, but only to defend yourself, and in a way that takes the person down quickly so that you can get the hell out of the situation, not take revenge. If a gun is ever involved, though, you only shoot if you are going to shoot to kill, otherwise you don't even point the gun near a person. And you only point it if there is no other option. Dad will teach you how to shoot, not because taking the life of any living thing is cool or even acceptable unless it's for survival, but because guns kill when people don't know how to use them. Plus, if a gun makes its way into your hand in a life or death situation, you better know what to do.

Sorry to harp on all of this, but knowing that you will be under emotional or physical distress and I may not be there to protect you gets me a little spun up. Just be careful. Be cautious and have the tools that you will need to face any situation, and you will be okay. That's all you can do.

3. There is always a silver lining, it's just hard to find sometimes. Devoting energy to finding that lining rather than agonizing over what you cannot change often helps.

My diagnosis in 2005 was devastating. Not only did I have my back split in two and bone sawed away, but the illusion of immortality was taken from me. Everything I thought I knew about my future was called into question. The potential loss of my legs, knowing that the cancer would most likely come back someday, and the likelihood that I would never be able to have children all sent my mind spinning. The physical pain was indescribable, but was dwarfed by the emotional pain and grief. But the self-discovery exceeded both, and today I am a much better doctor than I ever could have dreamed of being if I hadn't suffered illness and survived.

I often see people at their most terrified and devastated. Giving people diagnoses of fatal conditions is an unfortunate part of my job. But because of what I have been through, I can speak from experience and help people find the strength to get through the shock and muster the strength to deal with the news. The strength is theirs and I have only a minor role, but I have had many patients tell me what a difference it made to hear the perspective of a survivor. Illness is extremely isolating, and feeling like you have people around you that have been through similar experiences helps to alleviate the horror a little.

Every time I hear from one of my patients that my perspective has helped them get through the first days of their diagnosis, or see their families' faces regain a little color after I sit with them and explain the nature of the disease and the emotional beast that is upon them, I feel relief from my own burden. Somehow, even though my words likely make my patients' and their families' fears even more concrete, having some sense of understanding what is going on, and some validation of their plight makes it more tolerable. And seeing their relief does that same thing for me.

I have even had the recurrent ridiculous thought that maybe my cancer was a good thing. After all, it has certainly made me a better and more selfless person, and certainly happier due to newfound perspective. The thought is of course still obscenely ridiculous. I am making the best of the positives that have come from a horrible diagnosis that has set in motion a series of events that culminates in the very reason that I am writing this to you, the inevitability and potential immediacy of my own death.

It was a lot easier to rationalize my tumult before you came along. I always wanted kids and knew that I would love it, but I never knew that your smile would touch my soul. I know it has probably been said by many and sounds trite, but watching you smile and learn and laugh and play makes me want to cling to this Earth more than I ever wanted to before. Knowing that my absence will cause you pain makes me loathe my diagnosis all the more. It makes any thought of worthwhile purpose to the injustice of my illness laughable. But I have to remember how I came to be the person that is your mom.

Finding the silver lining has become a forte of mine, largely out of necessity given my saga of unfortunate medical events. But it is a strength that I cherish nonetheless. Good can always come from bad. You just have to find the good, refuse to let the bad win. With tragedy comes loss. The pain is there. There is nothing we can do to undo it. But we can shape what comes from it. We can refuse to let it own us, and cherish the joys that made that loss so unbearable.

One such loss for me was losing Joe. He was an odd combination of wonderful friend and father figure for me, and a man that was filled with brightness. He was not only incredibly smart, but kind, goodwilled, goodhearted, and ridiculously fun. I love him beyond measure and still feel the devastation of his loss. I still, more than two years after his death, break down crying while driving sometimes. But, though the world is a worse place without him, it is a far better place than it would have been if he had never been in it. His loss is only so great because of all of the wonderful times I shared with him.

Watching him and Elaine raise Anna and Duncan was inspirational. They were such incredibly loving parents and respected their kids as individuals as long as I have known them. Anna's purple hair was not a betrayal of them, but an expression of herself. Duncan's track meets hours away were privileges to attend for them, never cursed obligations. It was refreshing. And watching Joe and Elaine together was what love stories try to capture. Their mutual love, respect, and trust seeped from every pore when they looked at each other.

I cannot imagine the loss that Joe's family feels now that he is no longer physically here, but I know that I would not trade my pain for anything in this world. I got to know him, and for that I will gladly pay whatever price is asked of me. More than that, I still have Elaine, Dunk, and Anna, not to mention all of the other wonderful friends and family in my life. Life is unpredictable, so I do my best to cherish those I love while I am still here and be thankful for the opportunity.

We all inevitably suffer loss in our lives. All we can do is learn to cope with the pain or be consumed by it. I was relieved to find that there is more joy to be gained from using my own pain to lessen that of others than I had realized. I will always savor the sweet despair of having known Joe. And though my time may well end before I would like, I got to make you, Casey, and for that I could not be more proud or grateful.

If you are reading this because I am gone, I am truly sorry. I cannot imagine the loss you will feel in not getting to grow up with a mother. I hope that this at least provides you with some sense of who I was and how much I love you. And I hope that you can take that loss and apply it to a constructive purpose. I think it will give you a great deal of relief and will make some sense of the injustice of my absence.

4. There are so many people that love you and would do anything for you, and it isn't just because our family and friends love me and want to help.

You have had a spark since the day you were born, and people are inevitably drawn to it. You originated on the day that Joe passed away (as I mentioned, I found out the next morning). I can't help but see some of his impish kindness in your eyes, even if it's just because he did such a good job nourishing it in me. I prefer to think that his spirit made its way to you in some way, though. You and he share this amazing positivity that brightens the world around you without being false.

Regardless of the parts of me, your dad, and all of those that have influenced us along the way that shine forth through you, you are purely you. Never let anyone else take ownership of you or your actions. No one else can determine who or what you should be, and any efforts to let others decide (or to defy them) will only start you on an inherently conflicting path. That being said, not everything you do has to be profound or launching you on some important journey. Sometimes it is painfully unclear which path to take, or even where the paths lie. When that happens, just stop and think about what you truly enjoy and brainstorm about associated opportunities.

For instance, you already adore animals. A dog passes by, or appears on the TV screen, and nothing else matters. You smile, yell, point, and do everything within your power to make your way closer. So, say money is really tight at some point, and you decide that you need to make some cash. Think about working at a pet shop, or a veterinarian's, or a dog wash. You may well find that there are things about it that you don't like, but figuring out which paths you do not want to take is often just as constructive as figuring out which ones you are interested in.

Life is largely a process of elimination. But remember that, you are not going to enjoy yourself all the time. Life is hard work, and therefore anything that we do in it will also require dedication, and usually entail some hardship. The question is, do you net happiness from the experience, and how low do the worst experiences take you? If the worst is tolerable and you gain more happiness than you spend energy laboring over the endeavor, then you are in a good place. If not, take stock of the skills and lessons that you have learned from the experience, and make preparations to move on. Sometimes this means looking for another type of job in the same field, the same job at a different location, or going back to brainstorming about what makes you happy and applying what you have learned to something else entirely. Whatever happens, you have gained the wisdom of experience and perseverance in the process.

Most importantly, though, do not worry about what other people want from you (until you start a family and become a team that has to work together toward common goals). What you do with your life is your decision, and as long as you are realistic about what the demands, sacrifices, and benefits will be, then you cannot go wrong. Along those lines, though, you do NEED a good education. Life becomes very difficult when employers don't have clear evidence that you can apply yourself to a goal and succeed. It is up to you to decide what it is that drives you, interests you, and where you want to carve out your niche, but that can only be done with a lot of dedication to learning AND obtaining credentials that prove it to those judging you for employment.

Who you are inside, and what you apply your energies to, are entirely up to you. Those that love you will be there to support you along the way. Unfortunately, no matter what you decide about those things, you will still need money. You may not need a lot of money. That is also up to you. You decide what things you need, how much space you really want, and how much travel (or other similarly expensive opportunities) matter to you. Once you determine that, then you can decide how it is you will get there. This usually means more schooling, internships, or other forms of training/education. Just remember, that though these things are demanding and may sap you of time and energy, they will provide you with the knowledge that allows you opportunity in the future.

There are more things than money that provide opportunity, including the people that you know and whether or not you have been willing to help them in the past, but money is the most powerful form of opportunity in this world, at least as it is now. Money allows you to help people, and yourself, when times get difficult, and that makes a huge difference when it comes to quality of life.

More than anything, I want you to have a happy and rewarding life filled with love. Those things are far more important than money will ever be. I just want to make sure you consider all of these things as you are deciding who you want to be in your life. Ease is a wonderful thing. It makes everything else all the more enjoyable, and money frequently, but not always, equals greater ease as long as you remember that love and kindness are never to be sacrificed in the name of money.

To Come...

5. People do let you down sometimes. We are all weak jerks sometimes. The key is that you learn from the experience and look hard at yourself to figure out why you did it.

6. We all get lost. Figuring out who we are is a long and winding trek. Surviving pain is what gives us perspective and allows us to reach out and help others. Above all, try to reduce regret.

7. If it's inappropriate but clever, it's funny; If it's hateful, it's wrong. All hate stems from ignorance and fear.

8. A degree does not equal intelligence, but it does a hell of a lot to help you get by in the world. And, with few exceptions, it really doesn't matter what you get your degree in as long as you enjoy learning about it.

9. All you can do is your best. Stressing out about whether you will succeed just wastes energy you could apply to your goal (I am a HUGE hypocrite, by the way :)

10. This is a big one: Every boy (or girl, whatever) you like will not like you. If you have to be anyone other

than yourself to win affections, everyone loses in the end.

11. Bad things happen. Sometimes they are so bad that we cannot fathom going on. The only thing that we can control is our own responses to the good and bad. The rest is out of our hands. A nap and/or hanging out with a good friend usually helps. Getting really drunk usually makes it worse: nausea + headache + sad = not helpful.

12. I'm sure it is no surprise to you at this point that mama was a lush. My dad taught me a very important lesson when I got out of control in college and was depressed and drinking too much. Alcohol is a food and a drug. If you ever get enveloped in your own need for it, you can't enjoy it anymore. And if you get to the point that you have to stop for your own emotional or physical health, you have lost out on a food that is so very diverse and complex that you will probably forever regret it.

13. Take care of your loved ones and be a kind stranger, but beware of people that have a need for drama and avoid those that always call but never pick up the phone.

14. There is never any excuse for hurting animals or children. People that take advantage of the weak and vulnerable are to be feared. They have no conscience.

15. Ideally, we hurt no one, but we must defend ourselves or those that depend on us for safety. It can probably be done with words. Try.

16. You can have a small amount of the richest foods anytime, as long as you are willing to do 5–10 min of abdominal exercises 5 days a week. A large amount of rich foods is a waste. Their novelty is the draw (and heavy foods make you feel like crap after a while).

17. You have a responsibility to yourself and those in your care to be moderate in your vices.

18. Pain, fever, and weight are harder to get rid of than prevent, but if they occur, it takes dedication and compliance with an organized health plan to get rid of.

19. People that love you appreciate your willingness to ask for help. It makes their job easier.

20. Always tip well. Share, especially the good stuff.

21. Find a way to love yourself, even when you are at your worst.

22. When you don't know what to do, tell your story to yourself. It will help you organize your thoughts and figure out where the decisions really lie. Be strong but caring in your response and pick the path that gets the suffering over with and leads to better things.

23. You can validate people's concerns without giving them what they want OR ask for.

24. When you tell people things that make them sad or mad, make sure you are clear on your own intentions.

25. There is not a person in the world, young or old, that you cannot stand to learn from and share your own knowledge with; the lesson that you learn from

them may not always be the one they are trying to teach you, though.

26. Know that I have never loved as I do you. Dream of me. I will be there.

Printed in the USA
CPSIA information can be obtained
at www.ICGtesting.com
LVHW022315210224
772324LV00002BA/4

9 798891 551084